This Ticket entitles

Ld Mansfield

to a Sight of the

BRITISH MUSEUM,

at the Hour of *One* on *Wednesday*

the *3* of *March* 1790.

No Money is to be given to the Servants.

This Ticket had been preserved by M.r Gough & was given

THE
BRITISH
MUSEUM
DIARY
2003

PERSONAL DETAILS

NAME ....

ADDRESS ....

....

....

....

....

TEL. (PRIVATE) ....

FAX (PRIVATE) ....

E-MAIL (PRIVATE) ....

TEL. (BUSINESS) ....

FAX (BUSINESS) ....

E-MAIL (BUSINESS) ....

....

NATIONAL INSURANCE NO. ....

PASSPORT NO. ....

....

BANK TEL. ....

CREDIT CARD TEL. ....

....

DOCTOR TEL. ....

BLOOD GROUP ....

NATIONAL HEALTH NO. ....

DENTIST TEL. ....

....

VEHICLE REGISTRATION NO. ....

MOTOR INSURANCE POLICY NO. ....

AA/RAC MEMBERSHIP NO. ....

....

IN CASE OF ACCIDENT PLEASE NOTIFY:

NAME ....

ADDRESS ....

....

....

TEL. ....

....

THE BRITISH MUSEUM

Great Russell Street
London WC1B 3DG
General enquiries 020 7323 8599
Access enquiries 020 7637 7384
www.thebritishmuseum.ac.uk

Underground stations
Holborn, Russell Square, Tottenham Court Road

Main line stations
Euston, King's Cross

Museum opening hours
10.00–17.30 Sat–Wed
10.00–20.30 Thurs–Fri (selected galleries only)

Great Court opening hours
9.00–18.00 Sun–Wed
9.00–23.00 Thurs–Sat

Bookshop opening hours
9.30–18.00 Mon–Wed
9.30–20.00 Thurs–Fri
9.30–18.00 Sat
12.00–18.00 Sun

Shop by phone
Freephone 0800 0850864

Shop online
www.britishmuseum.co.uk

British Museum services
Education service 020 7323 8511
Friends 020 7323 8605
Traveller 020 7436 7575

Departments
Ancient Egypt and Sudan 020 7323 8311
Ancient Near East 020 7323 8628
Coins and Medals 020 7323 8607
Ethnography 020 7323 8041/8044
Greek and Roman Antiquities 020 7323 8600
Japanese Antiquities 020 7323 8560
Medieval and Modern Europe 020 7323 8629
Oriental Antiquities 020 7323 8250
Prehistory and Early Europe 020 7323 8450
Prints and Drawings 020 7323 8408

250 YEARS OF THE BRITISH MUSEUM

On 11 January 1753 Sir Hans Sloane died in his ninety-third year at his Manor House in Chelsea, and was buried with some pomp at Chelsea Old Church on 18 January. Two hundred and fifty years later, in 2003, the British Museum, the Natural History Museum and the British Library celebrate his life and his enduring bequest to the nation.

Sloane's long life spanned almost a century of British history. He was born in 1660, the year in which Charles II was restored to the throne after the Civil War. Fascinated by natural history since his childhood in Ireland, he studied in London under the patronage of the botanist John Ray and the scientist Robert Boyle, and continued his studies in the France of Louis XIV. In 1687, as personal physician to the Governor, he accompanied the Duke of Albemarle to Jamaica, returning in 1669, a year after the 'Glorious Revolution' of 1688 when William of Orange and Queen Mary came to the throne. On his return to London he set up in practice at no. 3 Bloomsbury Place and prospered, later including among his patients the new Hanoverian sovereigns. A capable and fortunate man, if not in the forefront intellectually, he was elected

The garden front of Montagu House, the Museum's first home.

President of the College of Physicians in 1719 and in 1727 succeeded Sir Isaac Newton as President of the Royal Society.

Sloane was a collector on a grand scale, having particularly profited from his visit to the West Indies. In due course he filled his home with an array of natural history specimens, books and antiquities – both bought and inherited – and expanded into no. 4 Bloomsbury Place. His collection of rarities was one of the sights of London: among its visitors were Benjamin Franklin, Handel and Linnaeus.

In 1742 Sloane moved to his manor house in Chelsea. Here he continued to add to his hoard, with increasing concern about its future after his

Viewing the sculptures in the new gallery at the British Museum; J. Findlay, *c.* 1832.

death. His son had died in infancy and neither of his well-married daughters inherited his collecting mania. Sloane's first will was made in October 1739 and a number of codicils followed, leaving his collection to the King for the nation in return for £20,000 to be paid to his two daughters. Should the nation refuse then the bequest was to be offered in turn to a series of European academies after which it was to be sold. A number of eminent Trustees were appointed to oversee its implementation.

The Hanoverians at this stage were not particularly noted for their interest in culture. King George II was reported to have said dismissively that he doubted in any case that there was £20,000 in the Treasury. However, Sloane's Trustees, led by Arthur Onslow, Speaker of the House of Commons, were more persistent. After a series of negotiations with Parliament it was agreed that funds to purchase the Sloane collection should be raised by means of a public lottery; the Cotton family's collection of manuscripts, languishing since its gift to the nation in 1700, would be added to the new museum and £10,000 would be laid out to purchase the collection of manuscripts put together by Robert and Edward Harley, Earls of Oxford. A new Board of Trustees would be established. And thus the British Museum Act received the royal assent on 7 June 1753.

Of the scandalous conduct of the lottery much could be said and even today it is difficult to disentangle how many crooks, of high and low status, were involved in raking in the illegal profits. However, over £95,000 was raised for the Museum which enabled the Trustees to purchase Montagu House, a 17th-century manor house in Bloomsbury, in 1754–5, appoint a small staff in 1756 and open to the public on 15 January 1759.

This was a new type of institution. Although not 'national' in the sense that it enthusiastically collected national antiquities (that was not to happen until the mid-19th century), unlike major collections abroad the British Museum belonged not to sovereign, church, or private individual, but to the nation through Parliament. The Trustees were directed to ensure that it should be 'maintained, not only for the Inspection and Entertainment of the learned and the curious, but for the general use and benefit of the Public'.

The Trustees, at first adhering to a rather circumscribed definition of 'the Public', attempted to ensure that the London mob were kept well outside the forbidding walls of Montagu House, requiring that admission, although free, should be by ticket only, applied for in advance, and

that visitors were not to wander unescorted. There are, however, a number of contemporary reports which indicate that not only the elite gained admittance. At the beginning of the 19th century these restrictive rules were swept away.

The British Museum is the best-known museum in the world. Over the centuries hundreds of thousands of visitors have come to Bloomsbury and continue to do so, and thousands of staff have devoted their lives to its service. It would not have survived and grown without the assistance of private donors, large and small and – it should not be forgotten – Parliament, which (sometimes grudgingly) has over two and a half centuries provided valued support and expended large sums of money. No institution survives 250 years without stories to tell and strange events to relate. This diary, produced to mark the 250th anniversary, hints at some of them. Early acquisitions, recorded in the Book of Presents, are sprinkled throughout, a reminder of the erstwhile 'noble cabinet' from which today's British Museum, Natural History Museum and British Library are descended.

Above Holiday Time, 1873. (*Illustrated London News*)

Right The Reading Room in the Great Court.

	January	February	March	April	May	June
MON						
TUE				1		
WED	1			2		
THUR	2			3	1	
FRI	3			4	2	
SAT	4	1	1	5	3	
SUN	5	2	2	6	4	1
MON	6	3	3	7	5	2
TUE	7	4	4	8	6	3
WED	8	5	5	9	7	4
THUR	9	6	6	10	8	5
FRI	10	7	7	11	9	6
SAT	11	8	8	12	10	7
SUN	12	9	9	13	11	8
MON	13	10	10	14	12	9
TUE	14	11	11	15	13	10
WED	15	12	12	16	14	11
THUR	16	13	13	17	15	12
FRI	17	14	14	18	16	13
SAT	18	15	15	19	17	14
SUN	19	16	16	20	18	15
MON	20	17	17	21	19	16
TUE	21	18	18	22	20	17
WED	22	19	19	23	21	18
THUR	23	20	20	24	22	19
FRI	24	21	21	25	23	20
SAT	25	22	22	26	24	21
SUN	26	23	23	27	25	22
MON	27	24	24	28	26	23
TUE	28	25	25	29	27	24
WED	29	26	26	30	28	25
THUR	30	27	27		29	26
FRI	31	28	28		30	27
SAT			29		31	28
SUN			30			29
MON			31			30

July	August	September	October	November	December	
		1			1	MON
1		2			2	TUE
2		3	1		3	WED
3		4	2		4	THUR
4	1	5	3		5	FRI
5	2	6	4	1	6	SAT
6	3	7	5	2	7	SUN
7	4	8	6	3	8	MON
8	5	9	7	4	9	TUE
9	6	10	8	5	10	WED
10	7	11	9	6	11	THUR
11	8	12	10	7	12	FRI
12	9	13	11	8	13	SAT
13	10	14	12	9	14	SUN
14	11	15	13	10	15	MON
15	12	16	14	11	16	TUE
16	13	17	15	12	17	WED
17	14	18	16	13	18	THUR
18	15	19	17	14	19	FRI
19	16	20	18	15	20	SAT
20	17	21	19	16	21	SUN
21	18	22	20	17	22	MON
22	19	23	21	18	23	TUE
23	20	24	22	19	24	WED
24	21	25	23	20	25	THUR
25	22	26	24	21	26	FRI
26	23	27	25	22	27	SAT
27	24	28	26	23	28	SUN
28	25	29	27	24	29	MON
29	26	30	28	25	30	TUE
30	27		29	26	31	WED
31	28		30	27		THUR
	29		31	28		FRI
	30			29		SAT
	31			30		SUN
						MON

2002

January 2002
MON	TUES	WED	THUR	FRI	SAT	SUN
	1	2	3	4	5	6
7	8	9	10	11	12	13
14	15	16	17	18	19	20
21	22	23	24	25	26	27
28	29	30	31			

February 2002
MON	TUES	WED	THUR	FRI	SAT	SUN
				1	2	3
4	5	6	7	8	9	10
11	12	13	14	15	16	17
18	19	20	21	22	23	24
25	26	27	28			

March 2002
MON	TUES	WED	THUR	FRI	SAT	SUN
				1	2	3
4	5	6	7	8	9	10
11	12	13	14	15	16	17
18	19	20	21	22	23	24
25	26	27	28	29	30	31

April 2002
MON	TUES	WED	THUR	FRI	SAT	SUN
1	2	3	4	5	6	7
8	9	10	11	12	13	14
15	16	17	18	19	20	21
22	23	24	25	26	27	28
29	30					

May 2002
MON	TUES	WED	THUR	FRI	SAT	SUN
		1	2	3	4	5
6	7	8	9	10	11	12
13	14	15	16	17	18	19
20	21	22	23	24	25	26
27	28	29	30	31		

June 2002
MON	TUES	WED	THUR	FRI	SAT	SUN
					1	2
3	4	5	6	7	8	9
10	11	12	13	14	15	16
17	18	19	20	21	22	23
24	25	26	27	28	29	30

July 2002
MON	TUES	WED	THUR	FRI	SAT	SUN
1	2	3	4	5	6	7
8	9	10	11	12	13	14
15	16	17	18	19	20	21
22	23	24	25	26	27	28
29	30	31				

August 2002
MON	TUES	WED	THUR	FRI	SAT	SUN
			1	2	3	4
5	6	7	8	9	10	11
12	13	14	15	16	17	18
19	20	21	22	23	24	25
26	27	28	29	30	31	

September 2002
MON	TUES	WED	THUR	FRI	SAT	SUN
						1
2	3	4	5	6	7	8
9	10	11	12	13	14	15
16	17	18	19	20	21	22
23	24	25	26	27	28	29
30						

October 2002
MON	TUES	WED	THUR	FRI	SAT	SUN
	1	2	3	4	5	6
7	8	9	10	11	12	13
14	15	16	17	18	19	20
21	22	23	24	25	26	27
28	29	30	31			

November 2002
MON	TUES	WED	THUR	FRI	SAT	SUN
				1	2	3
4	5	6	7	8	9	10
11	12	13	14	15	16	17
18	19	20	21	22	23	24
25	26	27	28	29	30	

December 2002
MON	TUES	WED	THUR	FRI	SAT	SUN
						1
2	3	4	5	6	7	8
9	10	11	12	13	14	15
16	17	18	19	20	21	22
23	24	25	26	27	28	29
30	31					

2004

January 2004
MON	TUES	WED	THUR	FRI	SAT	SUN
			1	2	3	4
5	6	7	8	9	10	11
12	13	14	15	16	17	18
19	20	21	22	23	24	25
26	27	28	29	30	31	

February 2004
MON	TUES	WED	THUR	FRI	SAT	SUN
						1
2	3	4	5	6	7	8
9	10	11	12	13	14	15
16	17	18	19	20	21	22
23	24	25	26	27	28	29

March 2004
MON	TUES	WED	THUR	FRI	SAT	SUN
1	2	3	4	5	6	7
8	9	10	11	12	13	14
15	16	17	18	19	20	21
22	23	24	25	26	27	28
29	30	31				

April 2004
MON	TUES	WED	THUR	FRI	SAT	SUN
			1	2	3	4
5	6	7	8	9	10	11
12	13	14	15	16	17	18
19	20	21	22	23	24	25
26	27	28	29	30		

May 2004
MON	TUES	WED	THUR	FRI	SAT	SUN
					1	2
3	4	5	6	7	8	9
10	11	12	13	14	15	16
17	18	19	20	21	22	23
24	25	26	27	28	29	30
31						

June 2004
MON	TUES	WED	THUR	FRI	SAT	SUN
	1	2	3	4	5	6
7	8	9	10	11	12	13
14	15	16	17	18	19	20
21	22	23	24	25	26	27
28	29	30				

July 2004
MON	TUES	WED	THUR	FRI	SAT	SUN
			1	2	3	4
5	6	7	8	9	10	11
12	13	14	15	16	17	18
19	20	21	22	23	24	25
26	27	28	29	30	31	

August 2004
MON	TUES	WED	THUR	FRI	SAT	SUN
						1
2	3	4	5	6	7	8
9	10	11	12	13	14	15
16	17	18	19	20	21	22
23	24	25	26	27	28	29
30	31					

September 2004
MON	TUES	WED	THUR	FRI	SAT	SUN
		1	2	3	4	5
6	7	8	9	10	11	12
13	14	15	16	17	18	19
20	21	22	23	24	25	26
27	28	29	30			

October 2004
MON	TUES	WED	THUR	FRI	SAT	SUN
				1	2	3
4	5	6	7	8	9	10
11	12	13	14	15	16	17
18	19	20	21	22	23	24
25	26	27	28	29	30	31

November 2004
MON	TUES	WED	THUR	FRI	SAT	SUN
1	2	3	4	5	6	7
8	9	10	11	12	13	14
15	16	17	18	19	20	21
22	23	24	25	26	27	28
29	30					

December 2004
MON	TUES	WED	THUR	FRI	SAT	SUN
		1	2	3	4	5
6	7	8	9	10	11	12
13	14	15	16	17	18	19
20	21	22	23	24	25	26
27	28	29	30	31		

HOLIDAYS AND FESTIVALS

BANK AND PUBLIC HOLIDAYS (UK AND R. OF IRELAND)	2003	2004
Bank holiday	January 1	January 1
Bank holiday (Scotland)	January 2	January 2
St Patrick's Day holiday (N. Ireland and R. of Ireland)	March 17	March 17
Good Friday	April 18	April 9
Easter Monday	April 21	April 12
May Day holiday	May 5	May 3
Spring Bank holiday	May 26	May 31
June holiday (R. of Ireland)	June 2	June 7
Orangeman's Day (N. Ireland)	July 14	July 12
Summer Bank holiday (R. of Ireland and Scotland)	August 4	August 2
Summer Bank holiday (England, N. Ireland and Wales)	August 25	August 30
October holiday (R. of Ireland)	October 27	October 25
Christmas holiday	December 25	December 27
Bank holiday	December 26	December 28

FIXED ANNIVERSARIES AND FESTIVALS

January
1 Circumcision
6 Epiphany
25 Conversion of St Paul

February
2 Purification
14 St Valentine

March
1 St David
17 St Patrick
19 St Joseph
25 Annunciation

April
23 St George
25 St Mark

May
1 St Philip and St James
8 World Red Cross Day
9 Europe Day
14 St Matthias

June
11 St Barnabas
24 St John the Baptist
29 St Peter and St Paul

July
3 St Thomas
22 St Mary Magdalene
25 St James

August
6 Transfiguration
15 Assumption
24 St Bartholomew

September
8 Blessed Virgin Mary
21 St Matthew
29 St Michael

October
18 St Luke
24 United Nations Day
28 St Simon and St Jude

November
1 All Saints
30 St Andrew

December
25 Christmas Day
26 St Stephen
27 St John the Evangelist
28 Holy Innocents

RELIGIOUS FESTIVALS	2003	2004
Buddhist		
Paranirvana Day	February 16	February 6
Wesak (Buddha Day)	May 16	May 4
Dharma Day	July 13	July 2
Chinese		
Yuan Tan (Lunar New Year)	February 1	January 22
Christian – Western		
Epiphany	January 6	January 6
Ash Wednesday	March 5	February 25
Palm Sunday	April 13	April 4
Good Friday	April 18	April 9
Easter Day	April 20	April 11
Ascension Day	May 29	May 20
Whit Sunday	June 8	May 30
Trinity Sunday	June 15	June 6
Advent Sunday	November 30	November 28
Christmas Day	December 25	December 25
Christian – Eastern Orthodox		
Christmas Day (not Greek Orthodox)	January 7	January 7
Lent Monday	March 10	February 23
Easter Day	April 27	April 11
Pentecost	June 15	May 30
Hindu		
Maha Shivratri	March 1	February 18
Holi	March 18	March 6
Shri Ram Navami	April 11	March 30
Raksha Bankhan	August 12	August 30
Shri Krishan Janmashtmi	August 20	September 6
Navrati	September 27	October 14
Vijay Dashmi	October 5	October 22
Diwali	October 25	November 12
New Year	October 26	November 13
*Islamic**	*A.H. 1423*	*A.H. 1424*
Eid Al-Addha	February 12	February 2
	A.H. 1424	*A.H. 1425*
Al Hijra (New Year)	March 5	February 22
Ashura	March 14	March 2
Milad Al-Nabi (Prophet's Birthday)	May 14	May 2
Lailat Al-Isra wa Al-Miraj	September 24	September 12
1st of Ramadan	October 27	October 15
Eid Al-Fittr	November 26	November 14
Jewish	*5763*	*5764*
Purim	March 18	March 7
Pesach (Passover) 1st day	April 17	April 6
Shavuot (Pentecost) 1st day	June 6	May 26
	5764	*5765*
Rosh Hashanah (Jewish New Year)	September 27	September 16
Yom Kippur (Day of Atonement)	October 6	September 25
Succot (Tabernacles)	October 11	September 30
Hanukkah 1st day	December 20	December 8
Sikh		
Birthday of Guru Gobind Singh Ji	January 5	January 5
Baisakhi	April 14	April 14
Martyrdom of Guru Arjan Dev Ji	June 16	June 16
Birthday of Guru Nanak Dev Ji	November 19	November 19
Martyrdom of Guru Tegh Bahadur Ji	November 24	November 24

* dates subject to visibility of new moon at Mecca

Dates are provisional as many religious festivals are determined by an actual sighting of the appropriate new moon.

	Capital	*Currency*	*Dial-in Code*	*Standard time difference from GMT**	*Public holidays 2003*
AUSTRALIA	Canberra	Australian dollar	61	Perth + 8 Darwin + 9½, Adelaide + 9½ Canberra, Hobart, Melbourne, Sydney + 10 Brisbane + 10	January 1, 26; April 18, 21, 25; June 9#; December 25, 26
AUSTRIA	Vienna	Euro	43	+ 1	January 1, 6; April 21; May 1, 29; June 9, 19; August 15; October 26; November 1; December 8, 25, 26
BELGIUM	Brussels	Euro	32	+ 1	January 1; April 21; May 1, 29; June 9; July 21; August 15; November 1, 11; December 25
CANADA	Ottawa	Canadian dollar	1	Montreal, Ottawa, Quebec, Toronto – 5 Winnipeg – 6 Calgary, Edmonton – 7 Vancouver – 8	January 1; April 18, 21; May 19; July 1; September 1; October 13; November 11; December 25, 26
CHINA	Beijing	Yuan	86	+ 8	January 1; February 1, 2, 3, 4, 5; March 8#; May 1, 4#; June 1#; August 1; October 1, 2
DENMARK	Copenhagen	Krone	45	+ 1	January 1; April 17, 18, 20; May 16, 29; June 5, 9; December 24, 25, 26
FINLAND	Helsinki	Euro	358	+ 2	January 1, 6; April 18, 20, 21; May 1, 29; June 8, 20, 21; November 1; December 6, 24, 25, 26
FRANCE	Paris	Euro	33	+ 1	January 1; 21 April; May 1, 8, 29; June 9; July 14; August 15; November 1, 11; December 25
GERMANY	Berlin	Euro	49	+ 1	January 1, 6#; April 18, 21; May 1, 29; June 9, 19#; August 15#; October 3, 31#; November 1#, 19#; December 25, 26, 31
GREECE	Athens	Euro	30	+ 2	January 1, 6; March 10, 25; April 25, 28; May 1; June 16; August 15; October 28; December 25, 26
HUNGARY	Budapest	Forint	36	+ 1	January 1; March 15; April 21; May 1; June 9; August 20; October 23; November 1; December 25, 26
ICELAND	Reykjavik	Króna	354	0	January 1; April 17, 18, 21, 24; May 1; June 9, 17; August 4; December 24, 25, 26, 31
INDIA	New Delhi	Rupee	91	+ 5½	January 1, 26; August 15; October 2; December 25
IRELAND (R.OF)	Dublin	Euro	353	0	January 1; March 17; April 18, 21; May 5; June 2; August 4; October 27; December 25, 26
ITALY	Rome	Euro	39	+ 1	January 1, 6; April 21, 25; May 1; June 2; August 15; November 1; December 8, 25, 26
JAPAN	Tokyo	Yen	81	+ 9	January 1, 13; February 11; March 20; April 29; May 2, 3, 4, 5; July 21; September 15, 23; October 13; November 3, 24; December 23
LUXEMBOURG	Luxembourg	Euro	352	+ 1	January 1; March 3; April 21; May 1, 29; June 9, 23; August 15; September 1; November 1; December 25, 26
NETHERLANDS	Amsterdam	Euro	31	+ 1	January 1; April 18#, 21, 30#; May 5#, 29; June 9; December 25, 26
NEW ZEALAND	Wellington	NZ dollar	64	+ 12	January 1, 2; February 6; April 18, 21, 25; June 2; October 27; December 25, 26
NORWAY	Oslo	Krone	47	+ 1	January 1; April 13, 17, 18, 21; May 1, 17, 29; June 9; December 25, 26, 31
POLAND	Warsaw	Zloty	48	+ 1	January 1; April 21; May 1, 3; June 19; August 15; November 1, 11; December 25, 26
PORTUGAL	Lisbon	Euro	351	+ 1	January 1; March 4; April 18, 25; May 1; June 10, 19; August 15; October 5; November 1; December 1, 8, 25
RUSSIA	Moscow	Ruble	7	Moscow, St Petersburg + 3 Vladivostok + 10	January 1, 2, 7; February 24; March 10; May 1, 2, 9; June 12; November 7; December 12
SPAIN	Madrid	Euro	34	+ 1	January 1, 6; April 18, 21; May 1; August 15; October 12; November 1; December 6, 8, 25
SWEDEN	Stockholm	Krona	46	+ 1	January 1, 6; April 18, 21; May 1, 29; June 9, 21; November 1; December 25, 26
SWITZERLAND	Bern	Swiss franc	41	+ 1	January 1, 2; April 18, 21; May 1, May 29; June 9; August 1; December 24, 25, 26, 31
USA	Washington DC	Dollar	1	New York, Washington Detroit, Philadelphia – 5 Chicago, Dallas, Houston – 6 Phoenix – 7 Los Angeles, San Diego – 9 Honolulu – 10	January 1, 20; February 17; May 26; July 4; September 1; October 13; November 11, 27; December 25

* The times listed are affected by local arrangements for daylight saving time. In most cases this means that in summer, the time is one hour ahead of the local standard time given.

Not observed countrywide.

INTERNATIONAL DIRECT DIALLING CODES AND WORLD TIMES

To call from any of the countries listed below to any other, dial:
1. the access code for the country from which you are calling
2. the country code for the country to which you are calling
3. the area code (any initial 0 or 9 is usually omitted)
4. the subscriber's number

Dial 155 for the UK International Operator.
Dial 153 for UK International Directory Enquiries.

	Access code	Country code	Standard time difference from GMT*
Algeria	00	213	+ 1
Argentina	00	54	− 3
Australia	0011	61	
Perth			+ 8
Darwin			+ 9½
Adelaide			+ 9½
Canberra, Hobart,			
Melbourne, Sydney			+ 10
Brisbane			+ 10
Austria #	00	43	+ 1
Bahrain	0	973	+ 3
Bangladesh	00	880	+ 6
Belgium	00	32	+ 1
Brazil	00	55	
Brasilia			− 3
Brunei	00	673	+ 8
Bulgaria	00	359	+ 2
Canada	011	1	
Montreal, Ottawa,			
Quebec, Toronto			− 5
Winnipeg			− 6
Calgary, Edmonton			− 7
Vancouver			− 8
Chile	00	56	− 4
China	00	86	+ 8
Croatia	00	385	+ 1
Cyprus	00	357	+ 2
Czech Republic	00	420	+ 1
Denmark	00	45	+ 1
Egypt	00	20	+ 2
Finland	00	358	+ 2
France	00	33	+ 1
Germany	00	49	+ 1
Greece	00	30	+ 2
Hong Kong	001	852	+ 8
Hungary	00	36	+ 1
Iceland	00	354	0
India	00	91	+ 5½
Indonesia	001	62	
Jakarta			+ 7
Iran	00	98	+ 3½
Iraq	00	964	+ 3
R. of Ireland	00	353	0
Israel	00	972	+ 2
Italy	00	39	+ 1
Japan	001	81	+ 9
Kenya	000	254	+ 3
Korea, Republic	001	82	+ 9
Kuwait	00	965	+ 3
Luxembourg	00	352	+ 1
Malaysia	00	60	+ 8
Malta	00	356	+ 1
Mexico	98	52	
Mexico City			− 6
Netherlands	00	31	+ 1
New Zealand	00	64	+ 12
Nigeria	009	234	+ 1
Norway	00	47	+ 1
Oman	00	968	+ 4
Pakistan	00	92	+ 5
Philippines	00	63	+ 8
Poland	00	48	+ 1
Portugal	00	351	0
Qatar	00	974	+ 3
Romania	00	40	+ 2
Russia	810	7	
Moscow, St Petersburg			+ 3
Vladivostok			+ 10
Saudi Arabia	00	966	+ 3
Singapore	001	65	+ 8
Slovakia	00	421	+ 1
Slovenia	00	386	+ 1
South Africa	09	27	+ 2
Spain	00	34	+ 1
Sweden	009	46	+ 1
Switzerland	00	41	+ 1
Syria	00	963	+ 2
Taiwan	002	886	+ 8
Thailand	001	66	+ 7
Tunisia	00	216	+ 1
Turkey	00	90	+ 2
UAE	00	971	+ 4
UK	00	44	0
USA	011	1	
Detroit, New York,			
Philadelphia, Washington			− 5
Chicago, Dallas, Houston			− 6
Phoenix			− 7
Los Angeles, San Diego			− 8
Honolulu			− 10
Venezuela	00	58	− 4

When calling from Austria to western Germany, dial 060 followed by area code plus subscriber's number; to Italy dial 040; to Switzerland dial 050.

* The times listed are affected by local arrangements for daylight saving time. In most cases this means that in summer, the time is one hour ahead of the local standard time given.

TRAVEL INFORMATION

RAIL NETWORK

National Rail Enquiry Service   08457 48 49 50
24-hour service: national times and fares enquiries,
including boat and connecting rail services to Ireland

Sleeper reservations

ScotRail Railways	08457 55 00 33
Great Western Trains	08457 000 125

Europe

By rail and sea	08705 848 848

Eurostar   0870 160 6600

Channel Tunnel passenger service

JourneyCall UK*   0906 550 0000

Trains, buses, coaches

* calls charged at £1 per minute

AIRPORT PHONE NUMBERS

Aberdeen	01224 722 331
Belfast City	028 9093 9093
Belfast International	028 9442 2888
Birmingham	0121 767 5511
Bristol	0870 121 2747
Cardiff	01446 711 111
Dublin, R. of Ireland	00 353 1 814 1111
East Midlands	01332 852 852
Edinburgh	0131 333 1000
Glasgow	0141 887 1111
Glasgow Prestwick	01292 479 822
Humberside	01652 688 456
Inverness	01667 464 000
Liverpool	0151 288 4000
London City	020 7646 0000
London Gatwick	08700 002 468
London Heathrow	0870 0000 123
London Luton	01582 405 100
London Stansted	0870 0000 303
Manchester	0161 489 3000
Newcastle	0191 286 0966
Norwich	01603 411 923
Shannon, R. of Ireland	00 353 614 71245
Southampton	023 8062 0021
Teeside	01325 332 811

The Townley marbles displayed in the
entrance hall of 7 Park Street, Westminster;
William Chambers, 1794.

CONVERSIONS

To convert to metric, multiply by the factor shown.
To convert from metric, divide by the factor.

Length

miles: kilometres	1.6093
yards: metres	0.9144
feet: metres	0.3048
inches: millimetres	25.4
inches: centimetres	2.54

Area

square miles: square kilometres	2.59
square miles: hectares	258.999
acres: square metres	4046.86
acres: hectares	0.4047
square yards: square metres	0.8361
square feet: square metres	0.0929
square feet: square centimetres	929.03
square inches: square millimetres	645.16
square inches: square centimetres	6.4516

Mass

tons: kilograms	1016.05
tons: tonnes	1.016
hundredweights: kilograms	50.8023
quarters: kilograms	12.7006
stones: kilograms	6.3503
pounds: kilograms	0.4536
ounces: grams	28.3495

Volume

cubic yards: cubic metres	0.7646
cubic feet: cubic metres	0.0283
cubic feet: cubic decimetres	28.3168
cubic inches: cubic centimetres	16.3871

Capacity

gallons: litres	4.546
US gallons: litres	3.785
quarts: litres	1.137
pints: litres	0.568

Velocity

miles per hour: kilometres per hour	1.6093
feet per minute: metres per minute	0.3048
inches per second: millimetres per second	25.4

Fuel consumption

gallons per mile: litres per kilometre	2.825
miles per gallon: kilometres per litre	0.354

Temperatures

°C	°F
0	32
5	41
15	59
20	68
30	86
40	104
50	122
60	140
70	158
80	176
90	194
100	212

$$°C = \tfrac{5}{9}\,(°F-32)$$
$$°F = \tfrac{9}{5}\,(°C+32)$$

The Beadle of
The British Museum.

'The first words of

Wisden were . . .

"January 1, British

Museum closed"'.

(*Sheffield Telegraph,*
20 April 1990)

December 2002

MON	TUES	WED	THUR	FRI	SAT	SUN
						1
2	3	4	5	6	7	8
9	10	11	12	13	14	15
16	17	18	19	20	21	22
23	24	25	26	27	28	29
30	31					

January 2003

MON	TUES	WED	THUR	FRI	SAT	SUN
		1	2	3	4	5
6	7	8	9	10	11	12
13	14	15	16	17	18	19
20	21	22	23	24	25	26
27	28	29	30	31		

---

30 MONDAY

---

31 TUESDAY

---

1 WEDNESDAY — NEW YEAR'S DAY, HOLIDAY (UK AND R. OF IRELAND)
• 1779 Montagu House damaged by the Great Storm • 1857 Charles Newton begins excavations
at Halikarnassos • 1920 Establishment of the Research Laboratory •

---

2 THURSDAY — HOLIDAY (SCOTLAND) ●

2003

JANUARY

3   FRIDAY

4   SATURDAY

5   SUNDAY

'There must be more to the After-life than hanging around the British Museum!' (*Punch*, 17 November 1982)

6   MONDAY — EPIPHANY

'Sir Hans Sloan is an instance of the great power of industry which can advance a man to a considerable height in the world's esteem with moderate parts and learning.'

(Commonplace Book of Dr William Stukeley (1687–1765))

7   TUESDAY • 1890 Rudyard Kipling obtains a reader's ticket •

GIFTS 1770

"Three Nuts whose kernels are said to be a sure tho' slow poison: by Mr Bancroft"

8   WEDNESDAY • 1915 The composer Sir Edward Elgar obtains a reader's ticket •

January 2003

MON	TUES	WED	THUR	FRI	SAT	SUN
		1	2	3	4	5
6	7	8	9	10	11	12
13	14	15	16	17	18	19
20	21	22	23	24	25	26
27	28	29	30	31		

9   THURSDAY

February 2003

MON	TUES	WED	THUR	FRI	SAT	SUN
					1	2
3	4	5	6	7	8	9
10	11	12	13	14	15	16
17	18	19	20	21	22	23
24	25	26	27	28		

2003

JANUARY

10   FRIDAY — ◑ • 1880 The dramatist and critic George Bernard Shaw obtains a reader's ticket •
• 1997 Gift from Asahi Shimbun, facilitated through the Japan Foundation, for the Great Court •

11   SATURDAY • 1753 Death of Sir Hans Sloane, founder of the British Museum •

Sir Hans Sloane (1660–1753),
engraved by John Faber jun.
after a painting by Thomas
Murray, 1728.

12   SUNDAY

'His decay, says Birch, was very gradual, so that he would often say that he wondered he was so long alive: that for many years he had been prepared for death, and was entirely resigned to the will of God. He would sometimes add, "I shall leave you one day or other when you do not expect it". He was ill, according to the same chronicler, only for two or three days before he died, and his illness "seemed rather the last efforts of a naturally strong constitution than any real distemper". He was free from bodily pain and his mind was composed.'

(E. St John Brooks, *Sir Hans Sloane: The Great Collector and his Circle*, 1953)

2003

13 MONDAY
• 1867 Augustus Wollaston Franks donates the 'Franks Casket' •1927 Leonard Woolley telegraphs message reporting the finding of gold in the Royal Cemetery at Ur •

14 TUESDAY

The western elevation
of the King's Library,
constructed 1823–7.

15 WEDNESDAY
• 1759 The British Museum opens to the public (by ticket only) •
• 1823 King George IV announces the gift to the nation of his father's library (the King's Library) •
• 1861 Appointment of Dr Samuel Birch, first Keeper of Egyptian and Assyrian Antiquities •

16 THURSDAY

January 2003

MON	TUES	WED	THUR	FRI	SAT	SUN
		1	2	3	4	5
6	7	8	9	10	11	12
13	14	15	16	17	18	19
20	21	22	23	24	25	26
27	28	29	30	31		

February 2003

MON	TUES	WED	THUR	FRI	SAT	SUN
					1	2
3	4	5	6	7	8	9
10	11	12	13	14	15	16
17	18	19	20	21	22	23
24	25	26	27	28		

2003

JANUARY

17 FRIDAY • 1861 Appointment of Charles Newton, first Keeper of Greek and Roman Antiquities •

18 SATURDAY — ○ • 1743 Funeral of Sir Hans Sloane at Chelsea Old Church •

19 SUNDAY • 1686 Montagu House on fire •

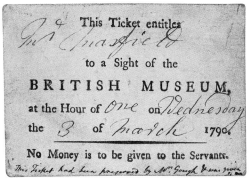

2003

20   MONDAY • 1998 Gift from Dr Raymond and Mrs Beverley Sackler for the Great Court •

21   TUESDAY • 1861 Appointment of W.S.W. Vaux, first Keeper of Coins and Medals •

22   WEDNESDAY • 1754 Meeting of the Museum's Trustees at the Manor House, Chelsea to inspect the Sloane collection • 1980 Inauguration of the New Wing •

23   THURSDAY

January 2003

MON	TUES	WED	THUR	FRI	SAT	SUN
		1	2	3	4	5
6	7	8	9	10	11	12
13	14	15	16	17	18	19
20	21	22	23	24	25	26
27	28	29	30	31		

February 2003

MON	TUES	WED	THUR	FRI	SAT	SUN
					1	2
3	4	5	6	7	8	9
10	11	12	13	14	15	16
17	18	19	20	21	22	23
24	25	26	27	28		

24   FRIDAY

25   SATURDAY – ☽

A foggy day,
in London town

It had me low,
and it had me down

I viewed the morning,
with much alarm

The British Museum,
had lost its charm

George and Ira Gershwin, 1938.

26   SUNDAY – AUSTRALIA DAY

'Of all the emotions that the British Museum inspires in the bosoms of the 3 million or so visitors who pass through its doors annually . . . awe must surely be the most frequently felt at least at first sight, love may, and often does, come at second sight.'

(Mollie Panter-Downes, *The New Yorker*, 21 January 1980)

27 MONDAY — HOLOCAUST MEMORIAL DAY

• 1753 First meeting of Sloane's Trustees at the Manor House, Chelsea • 1998 Opening of the Arthur I Fleischman Gallery of the Greek Bronze Age and Gallery of the Cyclades in the Bronze Age •

28 TUESDAY • 1890 Private view of the Museum galleries lit by electricity •

Electric light was installed in the exhibition galleries in 1890.

29 WEDNESDAY

30 THURSDAY • 1899 Gift of the Crystal Skull from the Christy Trustees • 1997 Opening of the HSBC Money Gallery with the aid of a £2 million gift from HSBC Holdings Plc•

January 2003

MON	TUES	WED	THUR	FRI	SAT	SUN
		1	2	3	4	5
6	7	8	9	10	11	12
13	14	15	16	17	18	19
20	21	22	23	24	25	26
27	28	29	30	31		

February 2003

MON	TUES	WED	THUR	FRI	SAT	SUN
					1	2
3	4	5	6	7	8	9
10	11	12	13	14	15	16
17	18	19	20	21	22	23
24	25	26	27	28		

2003

J A N U A R Y / F E B R U A R Y

GIFTS 1766

*"A dried Thumb dug up in
the foundations of St James's
Coffee House in August 1765:
from Mrs Rowles"*

31 FRIDAY

1 SATURDAY — ● • 1842 Visit by King Frederick William of Prussia •

'Mr Gray was unable
to arrest much of His
Majesty's attention to the
Zoology after he had
looked at the Painting of
the Dodo.'

(Diary of Sir Henry Ellis,
1 February 1842)

2 SUNDAY

'You will scarce guess how I employ my time; chiefly at present in the guardianship of embryos and cockleshells. Sir Hans Sloane is dead, and has made me one of the trustees to his museum . . . He valued it at four score thousand; and so would anybody who loves hippopotamuses, sharks with one ear, and spiders as big as geese! It is a rent-charge, to keep the foetuses in spirits! You may believe that *those* who think money the most valuable of all curiosities, will not be purchasers. The King has excused himself, saying he did not believe that there are twenty thousand pounds in the Treasury. We are a charming wise set, all philosophers, botanists, antiquarians, and mathematicians.'

(Horace Walpole to Horace Mann, 14 February 1753)

2003

ORDER 1764

*"That Dr Knight discharge
the upper or any of the other
maids, whose behaviour
he thinks improper"*

'A free Access to the
said general Repository,
and to the Collections
therein contained, shall be
given to all studious and
curious Persons.'

(British Museum Act, 1753)

February 2003

MON	TUES	WED	THUR	FRI	SAT	SUN
					1	2
3	4	5	6	7	8	9
10	11	12	13	14	15	16
17	18	19	20	21	22	23
24	25	26	27	28		

March 2003

MON	TUES	WED	THUR	FRI	SAT	SUN
					1	2
3	4	5	6	7	8	9
10	11	12	13	14	15	16
17	18	19	20	21	22	23
24	25	26	27	28	29	30
31						

3 MONDAY • 1817 Elgin collection opened to the public • 1830 Charles Dickens obtains his first reader's ticket •

4 TUESDAY

5 WEDNESDAY

6 THURSDAY — WAITANGI DAY, NEW ZEALAND

The Portland Vase, Rome,
1st century BC–1st century AD.

7 FRIDAY • 1845 The Portland Vase smashed by a student drop-out •

8 SATURDAY

9 SUNDAY – ☽

'On proceeding up to the Room where [the Portland Vase] was exhibited, I found it strewed on the ground in a thousand pieces, and was informed that a short time before a young man who had watched his opportunity when the room was clear, had taken up one of the large sculptured Babylonian stones, and dashed the Vase, together with the glass cover over it, to atoms! . . . This is the result of exhibiting such valuable and unique specimens of art to the mob!'

(Diary of Sir Frederic Madden, 7 February 1845)

GIFTS 1796

"A small Snake supposed to be a Boa: from Charles Townly Esqre"

10 MONDAY • 1933 The author Lawrence Durrell obtains a reader's ticket •

11 TUESDAY

GIFTS 1853

"A large bone of a Reptile probably megalosaurus, from the Stonesfield Oolite: from Lord Alfred Churchill"

12 WEDNESDAY

13 THURSDAY • 1980 Opening of 'The Vikings' exhibition by HM The Queen •

February 2003

MON	TUES	WED	THUR	FRI	SAT	SUN
					1	2
3	4	5	6	7	8	9
10	11	12	13	14	15	16
17	18	19	20	21	22	23
24	25	26	27	28		

March 2003

MON	TUES	WED	THUR	FRI	SAT	SUN
					1	2
3	4	5	6	7	8	9
10	11	12	13	14	15	16
17	18	19	20	21	22	23
24	25	26	27	28	29	30
31						

GIFTS 1760

*"Part of the Trunk of a tree,
as gnawed asunder by the Beaver:
from Capt. Mead"*

14 FRIDAY — ST VALENTINE

REPORT 1765

*"That part of the iron spikes
upon the wall at the West end
of the great Tarras in the garden
had been stole"*

15 SATURDAY

16 SUNDAY — ○

Replica of a Viking ship on the front lawn, 1980.

2003

FEBRUARY

17 MONDAY

---

18 TUESDAY

19 WEDNESDAY • 2001 Gift of $2 million from the Kresge Foundation for the Great Court •

February 2003

MON	TUES	WED	THUR	FRI	SAT	SUN
					1	2
3	4	5	6	7	8	9
10	11	12	13	14	15	16
17	18	19	20	21	22	23
24	25	26	27	28		

March 2003

MON	TUES	WED	THUR	FRI	SAT	SUN
					1	2
3	4	5	6	7	8	9
10	11	12	13	14	15	16
17	18	19	20	21	22	23
24	25	26	27	28	29	30
31						

20 THURSDAY • 1846 Austen Henry Layard discovers the head of a winged bull at Nimrud •

2003

REPORT 1851

*"On Mr Oldfield's brother
and sister locked in the
Medal Room till midnight"*

21 FRIDAY • 1981 Acquisition of the Thetford treasure approved •

22 SATURDAY • 1927 The novelist Anthony Powell obtains a reader's ticket •

GIFTS 1756

*"An Egyptian mummy with
its coffin, and the hieroglyphics
painted separately on canvass:
bequeathed by
Colonel William Lethieullier"*

23 SUNDAY — ☽

'The Reading Room is so exceedingly damp, it has very materially injured [the Keeper's] health.'

(Standing Committee, 19 February 1779)

A lady novelist in the Reading Room waiting for inspiration. (*The Graphic*, 15 January 1887)

2003

24 MONDAY • 1879 First use of electric light in the Reading Room •

25 TUESDAY

26 WEDNESDAY

27 THURSDAY • 1928 George Orwell, author of *1984* and *Animal Farm*, obtains a reader's ticket •

February 2003

MON	TUES	WED	THUR	FRI	SAT	SUN
					1	2
3	4	5	6	7	8	9
10	11	12	13	14	15	16
17	18	19	20	21	22	23
24	25	26	27	28		

March 2003

MON	TUES	WED	THUR	FRI	SAT	SUN
					1	2
3	4	5	6	7	8	9
10	11	12	13	14	15	16
17	18	19	20	21	22	23
24	25	26	27	28	29	30
31						

28 FRIDAY

'There is certainly no Mine, or Treasure like this in Europe, from what I have heard from foreign Gentlemen; nor can such a one ever be compiled again unless by a Miracle.'

(J. and A. van Rymsdyk, *Museum Britannicum*, 1778)

1 SATURDAY — ST DAVID
• 1851 Appointment of Augustus Wollaston Franks as the first curator of the British collections •

2 SUNDAY • 1998 Work begins on the site of the Great Court • 1873 George Smith (1840–76)
arrives in Nineveh and subsequently discovers missing fragments of the 'Flood Tablet'•

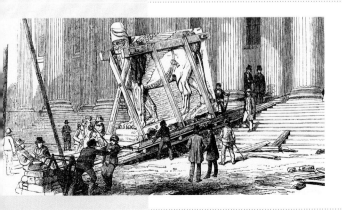

'The winged lion was brought from the Docks on a truck drawn by eleven horses.'

Arrival of the Assyrian winged lion.
(*Illustrated London News*, 28 February 1852)

THE
BRITISH MUSEUM
IN THE
EIGHTEENTH
CENTURY

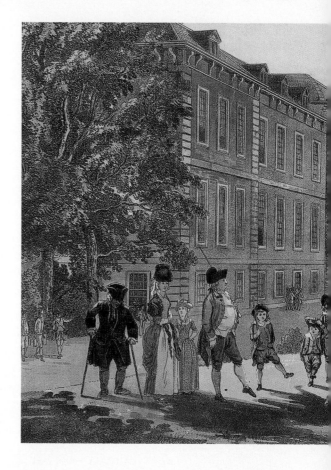

The 18th-century visitor would have made his or her way to Montagu House through the bustle and dirt of Great Russell Street on the edge of London. Tottenham Court Road led through the fields to the village where the Euston Road is now located; as today, there was a tavern on the corner of what is now Museum Street – previously the Dog and Duck, now renamed in honour of the Museum – a convenient drinking spot for the junior Museum staff who could also frequent the gin shops in the raffish streets and courts further south. Hawksmoor's church, with its steeple surmounted by King George II bizarrely dressed in a Roman toga, was a familiar landmark, having preceded the Museum by some twenty years.

A 'fine House & Pleasant Garden ... inhabited by Valuable Mss, Silent Pictures, & Ancient Mummies ... [with] A number of Learned and Deserving Persons ... made happy by the places bestowed on them to preserve & show this fine Collection', wrote Catherine Talbot on a preview visit to the Museum in August 1756.

The Museum from its first opening on 15 January 1759 was one of the great sights of London. Horace Walpole wrote, 'If you would see it, you must send a fortnight beforehand, it is so crowded'. In today's terms 'crowded' was rather an over-statement since the Trustees had laid down that only ten (later fifteen) visitors could be admitted each hour the Museum was open, and it did not open on weekends or on public holidays. On arrival at the forbidding front gate set in the steep outer wall of Montagu House visitors would be required to show their tickets of admission. They would be admitted by the

Porter, an imposing figure dressed in a 'gown of a plain drab colour, with a yellow tuft' brandishing a 'black staff tipt with silver' and escorted under the Ionic colonnade and across a courtyard into the main house to await the appointed hour.

From accounts by some visitors, the tours appear to have been conducted with great rapidity. The groups were initially allotted one hour in each of the three Departments (Printed Books, Manuscripts, Natural and Artificial Productions) and, as a bell rang, were passed from curator to curator. This was changed in 1761 to two hours allocated between the Departments as the visitors wished. The Department of Manuscripts and Medals early complained:

the [Department] ... is filled with company from nine o'clock in the morning, to one in the afternoon. During which Time, your two officers of the said Department, are to furnish Matters of Entertainment, and to answer all the Questions of forty different Persons, from the mechanic up to the first Scholar and Person of Quality in

The garden of the old British Museum,
Montagu House; Paul Sandby, 1780.

the Kingdom; who come all whetted with the Edge of Curiosity; and of whom, there are hardly any two that apprehend alike, or do not require the same thing to be represented to them in different Lights; or who would not be extremely offended, at any imaginary Incivility. The Fact is, that at the End of the four hours continued Attention and, if we may so call it, Debate; Your Officers of this Department are fit for nothing, but to Sleep or to take the necessary Alternative of Motion and the free Air. But, however fast the tour, a visit to Montagu House was a memorable occasion. The house itself was still magnificent for Ralph Montagu had spared no expense when it was first decorated. The main staircase was embellished with soaring frescoes showing Phaeton in his chariot. The visitor's first sight of the collections comprised a piece of the Giant's Causeway and other rock samples, Roman inscriptions and a Venetian genealogy. As the collections increased so new acquisitions would appear, not all of them curiosities. In 1778 the Otaheite Room opened with wonders brought from Captain Cook's voyages to the South Seas.

In the first room upstairs were displayed the Museum's Egyptian mummy and Egyptian statuettes. The visitor then moved on through rooms filled with a fabulous selection of natural history – stuffed birds and animals, rocks, corals, insects – creatures and plants they had never seen before. In the 18th century the tour would also include the library rooms where curators would, on request, bring volumes of printed books or manuscripts down from the shelves. The trail through the house concluded with a visit to a downstairs room where the Principal Librarian, Gowin Knight, showed his magnetical apparatus. Visitors would then be free to wander in the extensive gardens until dusk when the porter rang a bell ushering them out.

2003

ORDER 1757

"That no dogs be admitted

into the garden"

GIFTS 1779

"By Mr Thomas Lewis viz. part of

an Elephant's Tooth with a Bullet

init, and a pair of Eagle's Spurs"

March 2003

MON	TUES	WED	THUR	FRI	SAT	SUN
					1	2
3	4	5	6	7	8	9
10	11	12	13	14	15	16
17	18	19	20	21	22	23
24	25	26	27	28	29	30
31						

April 2003

MON	TUES	WED	THUR	FRI	SAT	SUN
	1	2	3	4	5	6
7	8	9	10	11	12	13
14	15	16	17	18	19	20
21	22	23	24	25	26	27
28	29	30				

3 MONDAY — ●

4 TUESDAY — SHROVE TUESDAY
• 1879 Oscar Wilde obtains a reader's ticket •

5 WEDNESDAY — ASH WEDNESDAY

6 THURSDAY

7 FRIDAY • 1978 Announcement of a new building for the British Library at St Pancras •

8 SATURDAY • 1837 King William IV grants the Museum's domestic servants the right to wear Windsor livery •

George Byard,
Senior Hall Porter,
in Windsor livery.

9 SUNDAY • 1753 Main Parliamentary debate on the Sloane collection •

'The ultimate salary of most of them [the Museum Attendants] was £120 per annum . . . and to supplement this they did various jobs in their evenings or on off days. Waiting at restaurants and social functions, ushering of sorts at theatres and elsewhere, and other similar work came their way. They would be found as extras in the refreshment tents at the Eton and Harrow and other cricket matches, in the ornamental uniform of attendants at the Royal Opera, Covent Garden, or even occasionally as footmen complete with livery, riding high through the London streets behind the carriage of some distinguished person in a civic or other public procession.' (William C. Smith, *A Handelian's Notebook,* 1965)

10 MONDAY • 1866 Establishment of the Department of British and Medieval Antiquities and Ethnography, Keeper A.W. Franks •

'Ordered, That the following words be added at the Bottom of the Tickets admitting Persons to a sight of the Museum viz. Persons admitted are not to touch anything.'

(Standing Committee, 21 March 1783)

BRITISH MUSEUM GARDEN TICKET,
FOR THE YEAR
1814,
ADMITS

11 TUESDAY — ☽ • 1757 Montagu House gardens opened to the public (by ticket) •

12 WEDNESDAY • 1996 Gift from Donald Kahn for the Great Court •

13 THURSDAY • 1837 Alfred, Lord Tennyson, obtains a reader's ticket • 1847 Acquisition of the Stanwick hoard with the requirement that a 'British Room' be provided •

March 2003

MON	TUES	WED	THUR	FRI	SAT	SUN
					1	2
3	4	5	6	7	8	9
10	11	12	13	14	15	16
17	18	19	20	21	22	23
24	25	26	27	28	29	30
31						

April 2003

MON	TUES	WED	THUR	FRI	SAT	SUN
	1	2	3	4	5	6
7	8	9	10	11	12	13
14	15	16	17	18	19	20
21	22	23	24	25	26	27
28	29	30				

2003

14 FRIDAY

15 SATURDAY • 1856 Antonio Panizzi appointed Principal Librarian •

The Principal Librarian
. . reminded the Trustees
hat the Act of Parliament
directing the disuse of
limbing boys for chimney
weeping would come into
operation the 1st July.'

(Standing Committee,
12 March 1842)

16 SUNDAY

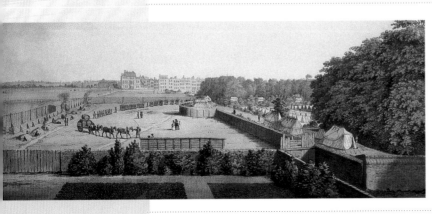

The York Regiment of Militia's encampment
in the Museum gardens following the Gordon
Riots of 1780; Paul Sandby.

17 MONDAY — ST PATRICK, HOLIDAY (N. IRELAND AND R. OF IRELAND)

18 TUESDAY — ○ • 1799 Appointment as maid of Mary Bygrave, aged 10 •

19 WEDNESDAY

20 THURSDAY • 1772 Parliament votes £8,410 for the purchase of Sir William Hamilton's collection of classical antiquities •

March 2003

MON	TUES	WED	THUR	FRI	SAT	SUN
					1	2
3	4	5	6	7	8	9
10	11	12	13	14	15	16
17	18	19	20	21	22	23
24	25	26	27	28	29	30
31						

April 2003

MON	TUES	WED	THUR	FRI	SAT	SUN
	1	2	3	4	5	6
7	8	9	10	11	12	13
14	15	16	17	18	19	20
21	22	23	24	25	26	27
28	29	30				

2003

21 FRIDAY

The staff . . . sometimes quirky, jealous, unworldly, occasionally fighting like cats and dogs among themselves, insufficiently paid, inadequately accommodated, but as a standard type immensely distinguished, learned and devoted.'

(Lord Radcliffe, *The Listener*, 21 March 1974)

22 SATURDAY

23 SUNDAY

'She had spent thirty and three years in the service of the Trustees, and though somewhat advanced in life, she still retained the remains of a beauty that must once have been very bewitchingly attractive. From my being the youngest man at that time in the Museum, she was particularly pleased with little attentions paid to her. I remember presenting her one summer morning with a moss-rose bud, when I remarked that at one time it would have done for an emblem of herself. She told me, with a woman's pride, that she was once rather attractive, at least the young fellows told her so.'   (Robert Cowtan, *Memories of the British Museum*, 1872)

Mary Bygrave, Museum housekeeper (d. 1846).

24 MONDAY • 1899 Death of Vincent Stuckey Lean and bequest of £45,000 for building King Edward VII's galleries •

25 TUESDAY — NATIONAL DAY, GREECE ◗

26 WEDNESDAY • 1832 William Makepeace Thackeray, novelist, obtains a reader's ticket •
• 1993 Parliamentary announcement of the Museum's acquisition of the Corbridge Lanx •

27 THURSDAY • 1882 Egypt Exploration Fund founded •

March 2003

MON	TUES	WED	THUR	FRI	SAT	SUN
					1	2
3	4	5	6	7	8	9
10	11	12	13	14	15	16
17	18	19	20	21	22	23
24	25	26	27	28	29	30
31						

April 2003

MON	TUES	WED	THUR	FRI	SAT	SUN
	1	2	3	4	5	6
7	8	9	10	11	12	13
14	15	16	17	18	19	20
21	22	23	24	25	26	27
28	29	30				

28 FRIDAY

29 SATURDAY • 1972 Tutankhamun exhibition opened by HM The Queen •

'The General Contents of the BRITISH MUSEUM: With REMARKS. Serving as a DIRECTORY In viewing that Noble CABINET.'

(Title of the first Guide book by Edmund Powlett, 1761)

30 SUNDAY — MOTHERING SUNDAY; BRITISH SUMMER TIME BEGINS; SUMMER TIME BEGINS, EU

'The Museum was opened today for the first time in the Easter holidays since it was founded and the result was really curious. The day being very fine, although cold, above 24,100 persons visited the Museum between 10 and 4 o'clock. The dust, heat and stench caused by such a crowd was intolerable. The Porters and Ticket-keepers had on for the first time the household dress of the King.'

(Diary of Sir Frederic Madden, 27 March 1837)

Holiday crowds visiting the Museum. (*Howitt's Journal*, 1847)

31 MONDAY

'Ordered, That Mr Keene be consulted about the best means of supplying the lead in the gardener's Toolhouse by some other materials not liable to be stolen.'

(Standing Committee, 6 April 1770)

1 TUESDAY — ● • 1988 Museum resumes responsibility for its buildings (ceded to Office of Works June 1815) •

2 WEDNESDAY

3 THURSDAY • 1754 Trustees' decision to purchase Montagu House • 1986 Opening of the Wolfson Galleries of Classical Sculpture and Inscriptions •

March 2003

MON	TUES	WED	THUR	FRI	SAT	SUN
					1	2
3	4	5	6	7	8	9
10	11	12	13	14	15	16
17	18	19	20	21	22	23
24	25	26	27	28	29	30
31						

April 2003

MON	TUES	WED	THUR	FRI	SAT	SUN
	1	2	3	4	5	6
7	8	9	10	11	12	13
14	15	16	17	18	19	20
21	22	23	24	25	26	27
28	29	30				

4   FRIDAY • 1874 The poet Arthur Rimbaud obtains a reader's ticket •

5   SATURDAY • 1755 Montagu House purchased for £10,250 • 1799 Death of Clayton Mordaunt Cracherode and bequest of books, engraved gems, coins, prints and drawings •

'Cracherode was accustomed for forty years of his life, to go every day to Mr Elmsly's in the Strand, and thence to Mr Payne's at the Mews-gate, to meet his literary friends.'

(*Gentleman's Magazine,* April 1799)

6   SUNDAY • 1753 Final Parliamentary debate on the Sloane collection • 1990 Opening of the Japanese galleries •

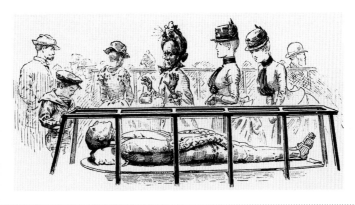

A Lady who thinks Embalming a cruel practice which should not be allowed. (*Illustrated London News,* 9 April 1887)

APRIL

7 MONDAY • 1755 The British Museum seal comes into use • 1891 Sir Arthur Conan Doyle, creator of Sherlock Holmes, obtains a reader's ticket. •

'Mr Panizzi wishes to know for his guidance whether the Trustees will allow cricket, foot-ball, hoop trundling, etc. to be played in the quadrangle in the Museum.'

(Officers Reports,
13 April 1861)

8 TUESDAY

GIFTS 1853

"Four rude iron weapons discovered at Winchester from Mr Drew"

9 WEDNESDAY — ☽ • 1994 Acquisition of the Hoxne hoard reported •

April 2003

MON	TUES	WED	THUR	FRI	SAT	SUN
	1	2	3	4	5	6
7	8	9	10	11	12	13
14	15	16	17	18	19	20
21	22	23	24	25	26	27
28	29	30				

10 THURSDAY

May 2003

MON	TUES	WED	THUR	FRI	SAT	SUN
			1	2	3	4
5	6	7	8	9	10	11
12	13	14	15	16	17	18
19	20	21	22	23	24	25
26	27	28	29	30	31	

2003

APRIL

The seal of the Trustees of the British Museum.

'The words '*publica munificentia*' [on the seal] were replaced by '*ex senatus consulto*'. No doubt it occurred to the Trustees that the purchase of lottery tickets could hardly be called public munificence.'
(19th-century Principal Librarian)

---

11 FRIDAY • 1807 Appointment of Taylor Combe, first Keeper of Antiquities •

---

12 SATURDAY • 1969 Establishment of Department of Prehistoric and Romano British Antiquities, Keeper John Brailsford •

---

13 SUNDAY — PALM SUNDAY

'The pensioners were snugly arranged in the new Manuscript rooms, with their pipes . . . with the ammunition close by them in open barrels, so that a spark might have blown them all up . . . and the attendants who were to stay, partly in the Hall, partly in the Large Manuscripts Saloon, where a good fire had been kept up during the day . . . And thus ended the memorable day of the 300 special constables in defence of the National Museum! I believe the soldiers would have been more than a match for the mob, but . . . the force inside very likely to have scattered like sheep.'

(Diary of Sir Frederic Madden, 10 April 1848 – defence against the Chartist rally in Russell Square)

14 MONDAY

15 TUESDAY

16 WEDNESDAY — ○ • 1660 Birth of Sir Hans Sloane at Killyleagh, Ireland •

April 2003

MON	TUES	WED	THUR	FRI	SAT	SUN
	1	2	3	4	5	6
7	8	9	10	11	12	13
14	15	16	17	18	19	20
21	22	23	24	25	26	27
28	29	30				

May 2003

MON	TUES	WED	THUR	FRI	SAT	SUN
			1	2	3	4
5	6	7	8	9	10	11
12	13	14	15	16	17	18
19	20	21	22	23	24	25
26	27	28	29	30	31	

17 THURSDAY

2003

APRIL

18 FRIDAY — GOOD FRIDAY, HOLIDAY (UK AND R. OF IRELAND)
• 1852 Antonio Panizzi's first sketch for the round Reading Room • 1881 Formal opening of the British Museum (Natural History) at South Kensington •

19 SATURDAY — EASTER EVE
• 1847 Front Hall, designed by Sydney Smirke and decorated by Collman and Davis opens to the public • 1902 V.I. Lenin obtains a reader's ticket under the alias Jacob Richter •

20 SUNDAY — EASTER DAY

Sale of material salvaged from the demolition of the Museum's old buildings, 20 April 1843.

Under the hive-like dome the stooping haunted readers
    Go up and down the alleys, tap the cells of knowledge –
Honey and wax, the accumulation of years –
Some on commission, some for the love of learning,
Some because they have nothing better to do
Or because they hope these walls of books will deaden
The drumming of the demon in their ears . . .

Louis MacNeice, 'The British Museum Reading Room'

21   MONDAY — EASTER MONDAY, HOLIDAY (UK AND R. OF IRELAND)
• Easter Monday 1837 – the Museum opened on its first public holiday •

22   TUESDAY

'Read a report . . .
that Hugh Henry,
Attendant of the Second
Class, had again been
found sleeping at his post
in the Assyrian Gallery.'

(Standing Committee,
23 April 1883)

23   WEDNESDAY — ST GEORGE   ◗
• 1827 Reading Rooms (now South and Middle Rooms) opened •

April 2003

MON	TUES	WED	THUR	FRI	SAT	SUN
	1	2	3	4	5	6
7	8	9	10	11	12	13
14	15	16	17	18	19	20
21	22	23	24	25	26	27
28	29	30				

May 2003

MON	TUES	WED	THUR	FRI	SAT	SUN
			1	2	3	4
5	6	7	8	9	10	11
12	13	14	15	16	17	18
19	20	21	22	23	24	25
26	27	28	29	30	31	

24   THURSDAY • 1824 Death of Richard Payne Knight and bequest of sculptures, bronzes, vases, prints, drawings, coins, medals and books • 1807 Sergeant's guard appointed to the Museum •

2003

APRIL

25 FRIDAY

26 SATURDAY

27 SUNDAY

A peripatetic art lecturer.
(*The Graphic*, 5 November 1881)

GIFTS 1758

"A petrified Crab from the East Indies: from the Hon Capt. Walpole"

28 MONDAY

29 TUESDAY

'Have you tried the famous echo in the Reading Room of the British Museum?'

(Gerard Hoffnung, *Misleading Advice for Tourists*)

30 WEDNESDAY — QUEEN'S DAY, NETHERLANDS

• 1896 The critic, novelist and poet G.K. Chesterton obtains a reader's ticket •

1 THURSDAY — ●

April 2003

MON	TUES	WED	THUR	FRI	SAT	SUN
	1	2	3	4	5	6
7	8	9	10	11	12	13
14	15	16	17	18	19	20
21	22	23	24	25	26	27
28	29	30				

May 2003

MON	TUES	WED	THUR	FRI	SAT	SUN
			1	2	3	4
5	6	7	8	9	10	11
12	13	14	15	16	17	18
19	20	21	22	23	24	25
26	27	28	29	30	31	

'The Reading-room of the British Museum is open to men and women of any country, or shade of political or other opinions.'
(*Handbook for Readers*, 1866)

2 FRIDAY • 1857 Party for the opening of the round Reading Room •

3 SATURDAY

4 SUNDAY • 1865 Death of Henry Christy and bequest of prehistoric and ethnographical collection •

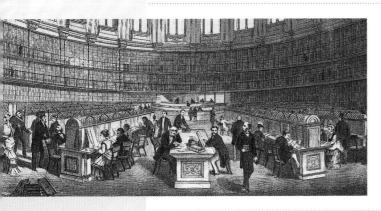

The Reading Room, architect Sydney Smirke.

GIFTS 1780

"An ancient British Flint Hatchet found under the soil of a Peat Bog, near Bigshot Lodge, in Windsor Forest: from the Rev Mr Burton of Oakingham, Berks"

5   MONDAY — MAY DAY HOLIDAY (UK AND R. OF IRELAND)

6   TUESDAY

GIFTS 1756

"Exotic trees of various sorts for the garden: from Mr Peter Collinson"

7   WEDNESDAY • 1914 Opening of King Edward VII's galleries •

May 2003

MON	TUES	WED	THUR	FRI	SAT	SUN
			1	2	3	4
5	6	7	8	9	10	11
12	13	14	15	16	17	18
19	20	21	22	23	24	25
26	27	28	29	30	31	

8   THURSDAY

June 2003

MON	TUES	WED	THUR	FRI	SAT	SUN
						1
2	3	4	5	6	7	8
9	10	11	12	13	14	15
16	17	18	19	20	21	22
23	24	25	26	27	28	29
30						

2003

MAY

GIFTS 1766

"A coined promissory note of General Macintosh of the kind with which he paid his Army in 1715: from Mr Milbourne of Newcastle"

9   FRIDAY — EUROPE DAY ◑

'Then we tot up figure
and figure

With arithmetical vigour –

Two and two make four –
or is it they are five?

We make bold experiments

With receipts and sales
and rents

Just to find out if the
Auditor's alive.'

Edward Maunde Thompson, The
work of the Director and Principal
Librarian, 10 May 1904)

10   SATURDAY • 1941 Upper western galleries, central saloon and south-west bookstack damaged in an air raid •

---

11   SUNDAY

Opening of King
Edward VII's galleries
by King George V and
Queen Mary.

12 MONDAY • 1999 Opening of the Roxie Walker Galleries of Egyptian Funerary Archaeology •
• 2000 Gift from the Henry Moore Foundation for the Sainsbury African Galleries •

'To enjoy this mighty building to the full, is to appreciate its nature in terms of its inmates as well as its architecture.'

(John Betjeman, 'Building the British Museum', in *Treasures of the British Museum*, 1971)

13 TUESDAY • 1823 Death of William White, donor of funds to erect the White Wing •

14 WEDNESDAY • 1996 Gift of £20 million from the Weston family for the construction of the Great Court •

15 THURSDAY • 1830 The author Washington Irvine obtains a reader's ticket •

May 2003

MON	TUES	WED	THUR	FRI	SAT	SUN
			1	2	3	4
5	6	7	8	9	10	11
12	13	14	15	16	17	18
19	20	21	22	23	24	25
26	27	28	29	30	31	

June 2003

MON	TUES	WED	THUR	FRI	SAT	SUN
						1
2	3	4	5	6	7	8
9	10	11	12	13	14	15
16	17	18	19	20	21	22
23	24	25	26	27	28	29
30						

2003

16 FRIDAY — ○

17 SATURDAY — NATIONAL INDEPENDANCE DAY, NORWAY
• 1756 Appointment of the first Principal Librarian, Dr Gowin Knight, submitted to the King •

18 SUNDAY • 1869 Laura Marx obtains a reader's ticket •

NOT TRANSFERABLE

THIS TICKET ADMITS

TO THE **READING ROOM** OF THE
BRITISH LIBRARY
AND THE READING ROOM OF
THE NEWSPAPER LIBRARY (COLINDALE)

FOR THE TERM OF

from............to.......................... (SEE BACK

'I am writer by profession I have sent to the British Museum from geneva, where I am usually living, two of my russian books (my pen-name is Iljin). I am now in London in order to study comparatively new english and new german philosophy . . . I should be very much obliged if you would give me admission ticket to the Reading Room of the British Museum.'

(V. Oulianoff's (V.I. Lenin) application for a reader's ticket 18 May 1908)

THE BRITISH MUSEUM IN THE NINETEENTH CENTURY

The mid-19th century visitor would probably have unhappy memories of the 1820s–50s, during which time the Museum was a building site, as Sir Robert Smirke's new museum arose and Montagu House was taken down. By 1853, however, the new bronze painted iron railings along Great Russell Street presented a much more inviting sight than the recently demolished wall of Montagu House. Bloomsbury was now entirely built up and the view across the fields to the north had gone.

Visitors could now cross the wide gravelled forecourt, climb the imposing steps and pass under Smirke's grand Ionic Colonnade surmounted by Westmacott's pedimental sculptural composition of 'The Rise of Civilization' with its blue background, into the brilliantly decorated front hall where Collman and Davis's scheme (recreated today) impressed those who were now aware that the ancient Greeks and Romans had painted their own buildings. The great staircase on the left was reminiscent of Montagu House. Robert Smirke had designed his new building around a large inner courtyard but this was visible only through a glass panel in the hall since, from 1852, the Museum had been brooding over the possibility of building in this space, and in 1854 work was to begin on Sydney Smirke's round Reading Room.

This was now a world-class museum compared to the near cabinet of curiosities which had been the early Montagu House. The public of all classes and ages (but still not babes in arms) flocked to the permanent exhibitions which were now open on public holidays, but still not Sundays. The require- ment to order tickets in advance had been removed in 1810. Visitor numbers had risen from around 15,000 a year at the beginning of the century to 300,000 or more and in 1851, the year of the Great Exhibition, two and a half million people came to the Museum.

Robert Smirke's imposing new Greek Revival galleries displayed the wonders of the natural and man-made worlds. During the 19th century the Museum had acquired the Rosetta Stone and other important Egyptian antiquities, the Parthenon sculptures, the Bassae frieze and Lycian tombs. British antiquities were just beginning to appear in a setting worthy of their importance and the realization of the antiquity

Polychrome decorative scheme for the Museum's front hall and main staircase; Collman and Davis, 1847.

of man could be discerned. Ethnography too was starting to make an impact and the natural history collection had expanded enormously. The public were afforded a brief glimpse of the magnificent King's Library in 1851 and in 1857 it opened permanently.

Behind the scenes much was going on and the professional curator was beginning to emerge. The invisible collections – coins and medals and prints and drawings – had expanded enormously. The first exhibition of prints appeared in the King's Library in 1851. Excavations of classical sites in the Ottoman Empire were underway and Austen Henry Layard was uncovering the wonders of the lost Assyrian empire. Augustus Wollaston Franks, the possessor of

a private fortune, was appointed in 1851, and he was to revolutionize the Museum's British, Continental, Oriental, Islamic and Ethnographic holdings.

One 19th-century guidebook author wrote of 'the bright new galleries of Sir Robert Smirke':

[The] mean precautions of the last century, contrast happily with the enlightened liberty of this. Crowds of all ranks and conditions besiege the doors of the British Museum, especially in holiday times, yet the skeleton of the elephant is spotless, and the bottled rattlesnakes continue to pickle in peace. . . . No attendant is deputed to dog the heels of five visitors and to watch them with the cold eye of a gaoler; no bell warns the company from one spot to another: all is open – free!

19 MONDAY

20 TUESDAY

21 WEDNESDAY • 1897 Death of Sir Augustus Wollaston Franks and bequest of a major collection of antiquities •

22 THURSDAY

May 2003

MON	TUES	WED	THUR	FRI	SAT	SUN
			1	2	3	4
5	6	7	8	9	10	11
12	13	14	15	16	17	18
19	20	21	22	23	24	25
26	27	28	29	30	31	

June 2003

MON	TUES	WED	THUR	FRI	SAT	SUN
						1
2	3	4	5	6	7	8
9	10	11	12	13	14	15
16	17	18	19	20	21	22
23	24	25	26	27	28	29
30						

2003

M A Y

23 FRIDAY — ☽

24 SATURDAY

'The [Restaurant] is
now a Public House
where cheeses, salads,
cucumbers and other
relishes for drink are alone
cheerfully supplied: the
calls incessantly are a "pint
of bitter" "a glass of mild"
"two pints of stout"...
(strange midday
refreshments for
students!). These calls
being loudly and joyously
re-echoed by the caterer.'

(Letter to the Principal
Librarian, 29 May 1865)

25 SUNDAY

'The Duke of Saxe Weimar, accompanied by his son, and two of the gentlemen,
visited the Museum. He arrived soon after eleven o'clock, and remained till past
three. He was chiefly interested with the Galleries of Antiquities and Mineralogy and
visited my Department last. Like all the rest of our royal visitors he seemed to care but
little about the Manuscripts and was perfectly ignorant of their nature and value. It is
useless to place treasures before such regal swine.'

(Diary of Sir Frederic Madden, 24 May 1842)

2003

'The trouble in settling
the Accounts of the
British Museum has of
late much increased.'

(Standing Committee,
26 May 1780)

GIFTS 1775

*"A Piece of Amber in which is
artfully inclosed a small Frog:
from Miss Mallorti of Fleet Street"*

26 MONDAY — HOLIDAY (UK)

27 TUESDAY • 1878 The novelist Thomas Hardy obtains a reader's ticket •

28 WEDNESDAY

29 THURSDAY — ASCENSION DAY
• 1689 Sir Hans Sloane returns to London from Jamaica •

May 2003

MON	TUES	WED	THUR	FRI	SAT	SUN
			1	2	3	4
5	6	7	8	9	10	11
12	13	14	15	16	17	18
19	20	21	22	23	24	25
26	27	28	29	30	31	

June 2003

MON	TUES	WED	THUR	FRI	SAT	SUN
						1
2	3	4	5	6	7	8
9	10	11	12	13	14	15
16	17	18	19	20	21	22
23	24	25	26	27	28	29
30						

30 FRIDAY

---

31 SATURDAY — ● • 1852 Front gates designed by Walker of York opened to the public •

'Mr Harper having to go out to a little Distance about seven in the Evening, thought he saw the Porter very drunk reeling along the Street.'

(Report, 31 May 1780)

---

1 SUNDAY • 1881 The British Museum (Natural History) opens to the public at South Kensington •

THE ZOOLOGICAL FAMILY REMOVING FROM THE BRITISH MUSEUM TO THEIR NEW HOUSE IN SOUTH KENSINGTON.

'Out with weazles, ferrets, skunks,
Elephants, come, pack your trunks;
You no longer dwell with us,
Yawning Hippopotamus.'

(*Punch*, 16 November 1861)

The Comic News, 18 July 1861.

JUNE

2 MONDAY — REPUBLIC DAY, ITALY; HOLIDAY (R. OF IRELAND)
• 1780 Start of the Gordon riots •

3 TUESDAY • 1756 Appointment of the first Principal Librarian, Gowin Knight •1808 Opening of the Townley Gallery by Queen Charlotte • 1999 Gift of £5.53 million from the Wellcome Trust for the Wellcome Gallery of Ethnography •

4 WEDNESDAY

5 THURSDAY — CONSTITUTION DAY, DENMARK

June 2003

MON	TUES	WED	THUR	FRI	SAT	SUN
						1
2	3	4	5	6	7	8
9	10	11	12	13	14	15
16	17	18	19	20	21	22
23	24	25	26	27	28	29
30						

July 2003

MON	TUES	WED	THUR	FRI	SAT	SUN
	1	2	3	4	5	6
7	8	9	10	11	12	13
14	15	16	17	18	19	20
21	22	23	24	25	26	27
28	29	30	31			

2003

JUNE

The British Museum Act 1753
and the Trustees' Mace.

6 FRIDAY — NATIONAL DAY, SWEDEN

7 SATURDAY — ☽ • 1753 British Museum Act receives the royal assent •

8 SUNDAY — WHIT SUNDAY

'His Majesty, attended in the state coach by the Marquis of Hartington, and the Earl of Lincoln went to the house of peers. . . . His Majesty being seated on the Throne, adorned with His Crown and Regal Ornaments, and attended by His Officers of State; the Duke of Cumberland, in his Robes sitting in his Place on His Majesty's Left Hand; the Lords being also in their Robes . . . the Clerk of the Crown read the Titles of the Bills to be passed.'

(Journals of the House of Lords, 7 June 1753)

2003

J U N E

9 MONDAY

10 TUESDAY — NATIONAL DAY, PORTUGAL

11 WEDNESDAY • 1808 Appointment of William Alexander, first Keeper of Prints and Drawings •

June 2003

MON	TUES	WED	THUR	FRI	SAT	SUN
						1
2	3	4	5	6	7	8
9	10	11	12	13	14	15
16	17	18	19	20	21	22
23	24	25	26	27	28	29
30						

12 THURSDAY • 1850 Karl Marx obtains his first reader's ticket •

July 2003

MON	TUES	WED	THUR	FRI	SAT	SUN
	1	2	3	4	5	6
7	8	9	10	11	12	13
14	15	16	17	18	19	20
21	22	23	24	25	26	27
28	29	30	31			

13 FRIDAY • 1903 Beatrix Potter obtains a reader's ticket •

14 SATURDAY — ○ • 1753 Tickets officially go on sale for the British Museum lottery •

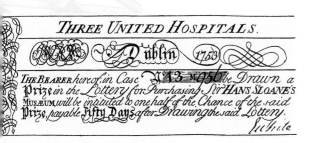

Ticket issued in the Dublin Hospitals Lottery on the results of the main (State) lottery.

15 SUNDAY — TRINITY SUNDAY; FATHER'S DAY, UK
• 1895 Oscar Wilde excluded from the Reading Room •

'On the 14th [June], when the Croud came on, there was an End of all Order, and Questions of every sort. . . . At about One of the Clock that Day, no gentleman would have wished himself in my Place for 150 £ which was my Parliamentary Allowance: People broke in, upon me, above me, behind me, and before me, and in at the Windows, with Ladders; the Partitions of my Desk were broke down, while I lay exposed to be plundered of all my Money, which was quite open.

(Testimony of Peter Leheup, Parliamentary Enquiry into the conduct of the Museum lottery, 1753)

2003

16 MONDAY

17 TUESDAY — NATIONAL DAY, ICELAND
• 1896 W. Somerset Maugham, novelist and playwright, obtains a reader's ticket •

18 WEDNESDAY • 1962 Duveen Gallery opens •

19 THURSDAY • 1820 Death of Sir Joseph Banks and bequest of an ethnographical and natural history collection •

June 2003

MON	TUES	WED	THUR	FRI	SAT	SUN
						1
2	3	4	5	6	7	8
9	10	11	12	13	14	15
16	17	18	19	20	21	22
23	24	25	26	27	28	29
30						

July 2003

MON	TUES	WED	THUR	FRI	SAT	SUN
	1	2	3	4	5	6
7	8	9	10	11	12	13
14	15	16	17	18	19	20
21	22	23	24	25	26	27
28	29	30	31			

20 FRIDAY

21 SATURDAY – LONGEST DAY ◐

22 SUNDAY

'So quickly was I conducted through this museum . . . that I saw merely the rooms, glass cases and book repositories: not the true British Museum. The visitors were of all classes and both sexes, including some of the lowest class; for, since the Museum is the property of the nation, everyone must be allowed the right of entry. I had with me Herr Wendeborn's guide-book . . . When the rest of the company saw that I had this book they gathered round me and I taught these English from Herr Wendeborn's book what they might see in their own museum!'

(Carl Philip Moritz, *Journeys of a German in England in 1782*)

2003

JUNE

23 MONDAY — NATIONAL DAY, LUXEMBOURG
• 1828 First books from the King's Library arrive in the Museum • 1982 Opening of the Modern Gallery •

24 TUESDAY • 1892 E.F. Benson, author of the Mapp and Lucia series, obtains a reader's ticket •
• 1999 Opening of the Chase Manhattan Gallery of North America •

25 WEDNESDAY • 1852 R.D. Blackmore, author of *Lorna Doone*, obtains a reader's ticket •
• 1928 Evelyn Waugh obtains a reader's ticket •

26 THURSDAY

June 2003

MON	TUES	WED	THUR	FRI	SAT	SUN
						1
2	3	4	5	6	7	8
9	10	11	12	13	14	15
16	17	18	19	20	21	22
23	24	25	26	27	28	29
30						

July 2003

MON	TUES	WED	THUR	FRI	SAT	SUN
	1	2	3	4	5	6
7	8	9	10	11	12	13
14	15	16	17	18	19	20
21	22	23	24	25	26	27
28	29	30	31			

27
FRIDAY • 1907 Foundation stone of King Edward VII's galleries laid by the King •
• 1991 Opening of Rome: City and Empire, the Wolfson Gallery of Roman Antiquities and
Italy before the Roman Empire •

28
SATURDAY • 1989 Opening of the John Addis Islamic Gallery •

GIFTS 1765

*"Two small Egyptian Urns
representing Canopus and Anubis
with a Marble Head of a Faun:
from Thomas Hollis Esqre"*

29
SUNDAY — ● • 1887 The poet W.B. Yeats obtains a reader's ticket •

'The room in the British Museum in which [the Keeper of Egyptian and Assyrian Antiquities] worked was . . . built over a section of basement containing apparatus connected with the heating of the Galleries, and the weird sounds which accompany the passage of hot water and steam through pipes, and the hissing of escaping steam, could be heard distinctly through the floor. Birch was firmly convinced that the engineer would one day lose control of his apparatus and blow the room and him in it up together.'

(Wallis Budge, *By Nile and Tigris*, 1920)

30 MONDAY

---

1 TUESDAY — CANADA DAY
• 1802 Gift from King George III of the Rosetta stone and other Egyptian antiquities •
• 1973 Separation of the British Museum and the British Library •

The Lion of Knidos
in the Great Court.

---

2 WEDNESDAY • 1846 Sir Robert Smirke resigns as the Museum's architect and is replaced
by his brother Sydney • 1999 Gift of £3 million from the Wolfson Foundation for the King's Library •

---

3 THURSDAY • 1989 First annual dinner for Patrons •

June 2003

MON	TUES	WED	THUR	FRI	SAT	SUN
						1
2	3	4	5	6	7	8
9	10	11	12	13	14	15
16	17	18	19	20	21	22
23	24	25	26	27	28	29
30						

July 2003

MON	TUES	WED	THUR	FRI	SAT	SUN
	1	2	3	4	5	6
7	8	9	10	11	12	13
14	15	16	17	18	19	20
21	22	23	24	25	26	27
28	29	30	31			

2003

'The British Museum and its grievances, like Domitian's turbot, can only be disposed of satisfactorily by a commission of senators.'

(*Civil Service Gazette*, July 1865)

4   FRIDAY — INDEPENDENCE DAY HOLIDAY, USA

5   SATURDAY

6   SUNDAY

'While he had been lying grovelling on the earth we had never seen his face at all; so that, when we had set him on his base, and our eyes met for the first time his calm, majestic, gaze, it seemed as if we had suddenly roused him from his sleep of ages.'

(Charles Newton, *Travels and Discoveries in the Levant*, 1865)

Charles Newton and the Lion of Knidos after its excavation in July 1858.

2003

JULY

7   MONDAY — ◑ • 1780 Prince of Wales and Prince Frederick visit the troops in the Museum garden •

8   TUESDAY

9   WEDNESDAY

10   THURSDAY • 1963 British Museum Act •

July 2003

MON	TUES	WED	THUR	FRI	SAT	SUN
	1	2	3	4	5	6
7	8	9	10	11	12	13
14	15	16	17	18	19	20
21	22	23	24	25	26	27
28	29	30	31			

August 2003

MON	TUES	WED	THUR	FRI	SAT	SUN
				1	2	3
4	5	6	7	8	9	10
11	12	13	14	15	16	17
18	19	20	21	22	23	24
25	26	27	28	29	30	31

2003

11   FRIDAY • 1823 Plans approved for Sir Robert Smirke's new building • 1995 Opening of The Hellenistic World: Art and Culture •

'At half past three the reigning Duke of Saxe Weimar, a lusty ugly-looking man, came to the Museum. . . . In the larger of the Manuscript Rooms His Highness broke a chair down with his weight. He was completely fixed in the frame.'

(Diary of Sir Henry Ellis, 11 July 1814)

12   SATURDAY

13   SUNDAY — ○ • 1993 Opening of The Raymond and Beverly Sackler Galleries of Later Mesopotamia and Ancient Anatolia •

GIFTS 1762

"A starved Cat and Rat from Mrs Cavendish"

A Museum cat.

14 MONDAY — HOLIDAY (N. IRELAND); NATIONAL DAY, FRANCE
• 1823 Ground broken for the construction of the King's Library •

'Mr Wyse said he had never heard that giving the humbler classes access to our national monuments was attended by evil consequences.'

(*The Times* Parliamentary Debate, 15 July 1842)

15 TUESDAY • 1905 Bram Stoker, author of *Dracula*, obtains a reader's ticket • 1997 Opening of the Weston Gallery of Roman Britain and the Galleries of the later Bronze Age and Celtic Europe •

16 WEDNESDAY • 1998 Opening of The Raymond and Beverly Sackler Gallery of the Ancient Levant •
• 1997 Gift from the Paul Hamlyn Foundation for the Paul Hamlyn Library in the Reading Room •
• 1998 Gift of £2.5 million from the Clore Duffield Foundation for the Clore Education Centre •

17 THURSDAY

July 2003

MON	TUES	WED	THUR	FRI	SAT	SUN
	1	2	3	4	5	6
7	8	9	10	11	12	13
14	15	16	17	18	19	20
21	22	23	24	25	26	27
28	29	30	31			

August 2003

MON	TUES	WED	THUR	FRI	SAT	SUN
				1	2	3
4	5	6	7	8	9	10
11	12	13	14	15	16	17
18	19	20	21	22	23	24
25	26	27	28	29	30	31

18   FRIDAY • 1991 Opening of The Raymond and Beverly Sackler Galleries of Early Mesopotamia and Egypt and Africa • 1997 Gift from Mr and Mrs Hugh Stevenson for the Hugh and Catherine Stevenson Lecture Theatre •

GIFTS 1765

"A Copy of the Printed Music of his son: from Mr Mozart"

19   SATURDAY

20   SUNDAY • 1911 The poet Rupert Brooke obtains a reader's ticket •

The motet 'God is our Refuge' composed for the British Museum by Wolfgang Amadeus Mozart during his visit to England 1764–5.

21   MONDAY — INDEPENDENCE DAY, BELGIUM ◗

'On the 19th of July, a young German, named Bittermann, had been detected by the Attendant Michie in the act of abstracting a glass eye from a stuffed Java Ox exhibited in the Mammalia saloon.'

(Standing Committee, 26 July 1879)

22   TUESDAY • 1857 Arrival of the Gorgon at Woolwich with sculptures from the Mausoleum at Halikarnassos •

23   WEDNESDAY • 1997 Gift of £15.75 million from the Heritage Lottery Fund for the South Portico and Clore Education Centre •

24   THURSDAY

July 2003

MON	TUES	WED	THUR	FRI	SAT	SUN
	1	2	3	4	5	6
7	8	9	10	11	12	13
14	15	16	17	18	19	20
21	22	23	24	25	26	27
28	29	30	31			

August 2003

MON	TUES	WED	THUR	FRI	SAT	SUN
				1	2	3
4	5	6	7	8	9	10
11	12	13	14	15	16	17
18	19	20	21	22	23	24
25	26	27	28	29	30	31

2003

JULY

25   FRIDAY • 1994 Opening of Europe: 15th–18th centuries and Europe: the 19th century •

26   SATURDAY • 1995 Gift of £6 million from the Annenberg Foundation and the Honourable and Mrs Walter H. Annenberg for the Walter and Leonore Annenberg Centre in the Great Court •

27   SUNDAY • 1972 British Library Act • 1998 Gift from the Peter Moores Charitable Trust for the Great Court •

'It was learned yesterday that the burial place of an early Anglo-Saxon chief, dating in all probability from the 6th century, had been unearthed in Suffolk. The body of the dead chief had been laid in a large rowing boat, which had been drawn up from the water and placed bodily in a deep grave. The grave dug for the reception of the boat had a length of 82 ft and a beam of 16 ft. Nothing remains of it but a pattern of iron clench nails in the ground but finds of considerable antiquarian interest accompanied the body.'

(*The Times*, 27 July 1939)

Helmet from the Sutton Hoo ship burial, deposited *c.* AD 625.

'It has been reported to the Director that the men in the Umbrella Pound in the Entrance Hall are in the habit of laying umbrellas, etc., or allowing them to remain, on the counter in such a way a to conceal the notice plate forbidding the offering of gratuities. This practice, if it exists, must cease.'

(Principal Librarian, 19 July 1927)

28 MONDAY • 1816 Removal of the bust of Ramesses II from Thebes begins •

29 TUESDAY – ●

30 WEDNESDAY

31 THURSDAY

July 2003

MON	TUES	WED	THUR	FRI	SAT	SUN
	1	2	3	4	5	6
7	8	9	10	11	12	13
14	15	16	17	18	19	20
21	22	23	24	25	26	27
28	29	30	31			

August 2003

MON	TUES	WED	THUR	FRI	SAT	SUN
				1	2	3
4	5	6	7	8	9	10
11	12	13	14	15	16	17
18	19	20	21	22	23	24
25	26	27	28	29	30	31

GIFTS 1766

*"A Busto in Terracotta of Madame
du Boccage the French translator
of Milton: Presented by herself"*

1

FRIDAY — NATIONAL DAY, SWITZERLAND

• 1984 Discovery of Lindow Man in a peat bog in Cheshire (Lindow Moss) • 1899 The dancer
Isadora Duncan obtains a reader's ticket •

2

SATURDAY • 1889 Arnold Bennett obtains a reader's ticket • 2000 Gift from the Honourable
Simon Sainsbury for the King's Library •

GIFTS 1767

*"The bones of an animal
(supposed to be an Elephant)
found on the Banks of the River
Ohio: from the Earl of Shelburne"*

3

SUNDAY

The removal of the bust of Ramesses II
in 1816 from the Ramesseum at Thebes;
Giovanni Battista Belzoni.

THE
BRITISH MUSEUM
IN THE
TWENTIETH CENTURY

The year 1953, the 200th anniversary of the Museum's foundation, was a time of both optimism and gloom. The Museum had still not recovered from the depression and under-funding of the 1930s, the dispersion of its collections to places of safety during the Second World War and the major damage to the western galleries, main staircase and south-west book stack caused by an incendiary raid in May 1941. For many years after the War, if it rained, staff walking through the upper western galleries had, in the absence of a roof, to carry umbrellas.

The celebration was marked by the publication of two books and a number of articles on Sir Hans Sloane and his collections and, for the staff, a party in the unreconstructed Assyrian basement. The universal ideals of its 18th-century founders had been set aside by the transfer to South Kensington in the 1880s of the natural history collections. The books and manuscripts were to follow administratively with the foundation of the British Library as a separate organization in 1973, and physically with the Library's removal to a new building at St Pancras in the 1990s.

The Museum's horizons had broadened from the 19th-century concern with Classical, Egyptian and Assyrian material and it now collected from all over the world. The Ethnography department had vastly increased in size, so much so that in 1970 it moved temporarily to the Museum of Mankind in Burlington Gardens. The British and other European collections filled galleries which at one time were occupied by natural history. A new building – King Edward VII's galleries, designed by the architect Sir John Burnet – had opened in 1914 fronting Montague Place.

In the centre of the courtyard was the thriving Reading Room – a library of last resort – which in the past hundred years had welcomed most of the great writers in English, politicians, musicians, and others of note. Its collections, now numbering many millions of books, were increasing at the rate of around 50,000 volumes a year and pressure for a move elsewhere had become acute.

Opposite the gates, the Museum Tavern survived but the rest of Bloomsbury had changed as small cafes and antiquarian bookshops had sprung up to cater for readers and other visitors. The Victorian 'rookery' to the south had long gone with road improvements of the early 20th century but Bloomsbury remained to some extent a residential area with butchers' and greengrocers' shops.

The exhibition galleries mid-century were in some instances rather dour. There was little provision for schoolchildren. Angus Wilson, the novelist, who was a member of staff from 1937 to 1955, wrote:

If the galleries were domestic housing it could be said that they range from the dowdy seaside lodging house of the manuscript display rooms, with their excess of dingy green sun-blinds that somehow suggest high tea and smells of boiled cabbage, through the phonily daring council house 'contemporary' dark blue ceiling of the Indian exhibition, to the sheer slum crowding of the Ethnographical galleries.

But there were better days ahead. The Parthenon sculptures would be displayed in their new gallery in 1962. Remodelling of the Assyrian and Classical sculpture galleries was to take place in the late 1960s/early 1970s and the Egyptian Sculpture Gallery was transformed in 1981. Other displays were revived and rearranged. A publications company was set up in 1973 and an Education Service established, and the Museum began to be more welcoming to visitors. In 1980 the 'New Wing' provided the first purpose-built restaurant and exhibition gallery.

A 20th-century artist sketches an Ancient Egyptian statue.

'With the exception of St Paul's Cathedral, perhaps no public building in London is more generally visited than the British Museum . . . It possesses two very great attractions; one, that it has much within it deserving attention; the other, that it may be seen for nothing.'

(*Old Humphrey's Walks in London*)

4 MONDAY — HOLIDAY (SCOTLAND AND R. OF IRELAND)

5 TUESDAY — ◗

6 WEDNESDAY • 1757 Letters patent by King George II donating the Old Royal Library of the sovereigns of England •

7 THURSDAY

August 2003

MON	TUES	WED	THUR	FRI	SAT	SUN
				1	2	3
4	5	6	7	8	9	10
11	12	13	14	15	16	17
18	19	20	21	22	23	24
25	26	27	28	29	30	31

September 2003

MON	TUES	WED	THUR	FRI	SAT	SUN
1	2	3	4	5	6	7
8	9	10	11	12	13	14
15	16	17	18	19	20	21
22	23	24	25	26	27	28
29	30					

8   FRIDAY

9   SATURDAY

10   SUNDAY • 1780 Departure of the York Regiment of Militia •

The Boy who breathed on the glass in the British Museum (detail); H.M. Bateman, 1916.

11 MONDAY

12 TUESDAY — ○ • 1802 Arrival of the first 'Elgin marbles' in England •

Thomas Bruce,
seventh Earl of Elgin;
G.P. Harding after
Anton Graff, c. 1795.

13 WEDNESDAY

August 2003

MON	TUES	WED	THUR	FRI	SAT	SUN
				1	2	3
4	5	6	7	8	9	10
11	12	13	14	15	16	17
18	19	20	21	22	23	24
25	26	27	28	29	30	31

September 2003

MON	TUES	WED	THUR	FRI	SAT	SUN
1	2	3	4	5	6	7
8	9	10	11	12	13	14
15	16	17	18	19	20	21
22	23	24	25	26	27	28
29	30					

14 THURSDAY • 1939 Coroner's inquest on the Sutton Hoo treasure •

2003

AUGUST

15 FRIDAY

16 SATURDAY • H.G. Wells obtains a reader's ticket •

17 SUNDAY

The Trustees in the temporary Elgin Room; A. Archer, 1819.

18 MONDAY

'A labourer who might be employed at 18/0d. a week would cost £46. 16s 0d. by the year. He will dust the cases badly and he cannot wash. The female servant in wages and board wages would cost £41. 14s 0d., and would add the washing to the other labour.'

(Principal Librarian, 1830)

19 TUESDAY

20 WEDNESDAY – ☽

21 THURSDAY

August 2003						
MON	TUES	WED	THUR	FRI	SAT	SUN
				1	2	3
4	5	6	7	8	9	10
11	12	13	14	15	16	17
18	19	20	21	22	23	24
25	26	27	28	29	30	31

September 2003						
MON	TUES	WED	THUR	FRI	SAT	SUN
1	2	3	4	5	6	7
8	9	10	11	12	13	14
15	16	17	18	19	20	21
22	23	24	25	26	27	28
29	30					

22 FRIDAY

23 SATURDAY
• 1894 The revolutionary Vera Zasulich obtains a reader's ticket •
• 1939 Evacuation of the collections outside London and to the Aldwych tube begins •

24 SUNDAY

'The Humble Petition of Dorothy Markland, sheweth that your Petitioner has liv'd in this House, thirty-two Years and as servant to the Museum, ever since the first Establishment of it, is now upwards of seventy-three years of Age, and is renderd incapable of doing her work having intirely lost her Sight, but by the kindness of Dr Morton she is allowd to keep her place; during life or as long as her Daughter can officiate for her.'

(Original papers, 24 August 1781)

The Museum maids; detail from a cartoon of 1833.

25 MONDAY — HOLIDAY (ENGLAND, N. IRELAND AND WALES)
• 1995 Gift of £4 million from Sir Robert and Lady Sainsbury, and David and Susie Sainsbury for the Sainsbury African Galleries •

'O rdered, That Mr Sheldon of Great Queen Street be permitted to examine the inside of some of the monsters of the Human Species.'

(Standing Committee, 28 August 1778)

26 TUESDAY

27 WEDNESDAY — ●

28 THURSDAY

August 2003

MON	TUES	WED	THUR	FRI	SAT	SUN
				1	2	3
4	5	6	7	8	9	10
11	12	13	14	15	16	17
18	19	20	21	22	23	24
25	26	27	28	29	30	31

September 2003

MON	TUES	WED	THUR	FRI	SAT	SUN
1	2	3	4	5	6	7
8	9	10	11	12	13	14
15	16	17	18	19	20	21
22	23	24	25	26	27	28
29	30					

2003

GIFTS 1766

*"The works of Dr Willian Harvey
in Latin, printed at London 1766
in 4o published and presented by
the College of Physicians"*

29 FRIDAY

GIFTS 1764

*"A pair of gloves made from
the beard of a shell fish found
on the Coast of Sicily"*

30 SATURDAY

31 SUNDAY • 1912 John Galsworthy, author of the *Forsythe Saga*, obtains a reader's ticket •

'Every afternoon, the opinion-sessions produce parades of objects, beautiful, bizarre or merely banal. It is too easy to doubt the value of scholars' labours on Amazonian nose-whistles or medieval latrines. But next time you want to know, "what is this?", you might be grateful for the return on our national investment in scholarship.'

(*Daily Telegraph*, 16 August 1988)

2003

SEPTEMBER

GIFTS 1780

"A young Humming bird with two heads and some vegetable wasps . . . from Mrs McLachlan of Norfolk Street"

'The Museum wore an autumnal aspect, as if built of petrified fog. The gilt statuary reclining above the bulging pillars provided the only gleam of colour. Pigeons stalked grumpily about, ruffling their feathers as if they felt the cold.'

(David Lodge, *The British Museum is Falling Down*, 1965)

1   MONDAY

2   TUESDAY

3   WEDNESDAY — ◐

4   THURSDAY

September 2003

MON	TUES	WED	THUR	FRI	SAT	SUN
1	2	3	4	5	6	7
8	9	10	11	12	13	14
15	16	17	18	19	20	21
22	23	24	25	26	27	28
29	30					

October 2003

MON	TUES	WED	THUR	FRI	SAT	SUN
		1	2	3	4	5
6	7	8	9	10	11	12
13	14	15	16	17	18	19
20	21	22	23	24	25	26
27	28	29	30	31		

2003

SEPTEMBER

5   FRIDAY • 1960 The poet Ted Hughes obtains a reader's ticket •

---

6   SATURDAY

---

7   SUNDAY

'Above all the British Museum pleased me best. . . . First we saw Egyptians that had been dead 3,000 years ago. Next we saw the skull of an elephant, and the Queen of Otaheite's hat, the crown is big enough to hold you, and the brim of it not much unlike the mat that lies at the bottom of our stairs.'

(John Coltman, age 12, in C.H. Beale (ed.), *Catherine Hutton and her Friends*, 1895)

2003

Cigarette card showing
Howis Wagner, baseball player
and non-smoker.

'If to collect cigarette
cards is a sign of
eccentricity, how then will
posterity judge one who
amassed the biggest
collection in the world?
Frankly I care not.'

(Edward Wharton Tigar, 1987)

8 MONDAY • 1823 First bricks laid for the foundation of the King's Library • 1981 Opening of the
refurbished Egyptian Sculpture Gallery •

9 TUESDAY

10 WEDNESDAY — ○

11 THURSDAY

September 2003

MON	TUES	WED	THUR	FRI	SAT	SUN
1	2	3	4	5	6	7
8	9	10	11	12	13	14
15	16	17	18	19	20	21
22	23	24	25	26	27	28
29	30					

October 2003

MON	TUES	WED	THUR	FRI	SAT	SUN
		1	2	3	4	5
6	7	8	9	10	11	12
13	14	15	16	17	18	19
20	21	22	23	24	25	26
27	28	29	30	31		

GIFTS 1776

*"A curious double Egg laid
by a Hen at Dunstable
from Lord Charles Cavendish"*

12 FRIDAY

GIFTS 1782

*"A shoe belonging to . . . [sic]
struck by lightning:
from Dr Pitcairn, President
of the College of Physicians"*

13 SATURDAY

---

14 SUNDAY

The King's Library, mid-19th century.

GIFTS 1780

"A Tiger cat from Senegal
from Joseph Banks Esqr"

15 MONDAY

16 TUESDAY

GIFTS 1762

"A copper medal of the Duke
of Cumberland on the battle
of Culloden from
Thomas Hollis Esqre"

17 WEDNESDAY

September 2003

MON	TUES	WED	THUR	FRI	SAT	SUN
1	2	3	4	5	6	7
8	9	10	11	12	13	14
15	16	17	18	19	20	21
22	23	24	25	26	27	28
29	30					

October 2003

MON	TUES	WED	THUR	FRI	SAT	SUN
		1	2	3	4	5
6	7	8	9	10	11	12
13	14	15	16	17	18	19
20	21	22	23	24	25	26
27	28	29	30	31		

18 THURSDAY — ◑

2003

SEPTEMBER

19 FRIDAY

20 SATURDAY

'The first floor consisting of twelve rooms, contains the Library of Printed Books. Strangers are not conducted through these apartments, as the mere sight of the outside of books cannot convey either instruction or amusement.'

(*Synopsis*, 1809)

21 SUNDAY

The gardens of Montagu House.

'The Inhabitants of the Houses in the Neighbourhood of the Museum with respectful compliments to the Trustees or Gentlemen resident there, Beg Leave to Represent to them that the Burning of the Leaves in the Museum Garden is such a Nuisance. And the Smoak and Smell arising from it are so disagreeable and offensive to the Inhabitants that they shall be exceedingly obliged to the Gentlemen if they will take it into their immediate consideration And give such orders to their Gardener as will effectually Prevent this Great Annoyance in future.'

(Original papers, 18 September 1784)

2003

GIFTS 1779

*"An extraordinary Egg laid
by a Hen three Months three
Weeks and three Days old,
from Mrs Blackmore"*

22 MONDAY • 1859 Drinking fountains erected by the front door •

ORDER 1786

*"A Portrait of Oliver Cromwell
with the Watch
that he usually wore: Bequeathed
by Sir Robt Rich"*

23 TUESDAY • 1994 Gift of £1 million from Chase Manhattan Bank for the North American Gallery •

24 WEDNESDAY

September 2003

MON	TUES	WED	THUR	FRI	SAT	SUN
1	2	3	4	5	6	7
8	9	10	11	12	13	14
15	16	17	18	19	20	21
22	23	24	25	26	27	28
29	30					

October 2003

MON	TUES	WED	THUR	FRI	SAT	SUN
		1	2	3	4	5
6	7	8	9	10	11	12
13	14	15	16	17	18	19
20	21	22	23	24	25	26
27	28	29	30	31		

25 THURSDAY

26 FRIDAY — ● • 1986 Gift of the library of the Royal Anthropological Institute •
• 1996 Gift of £30 million from the Millennium Commission for the Great Court •

'The tradesmen generally employed in this great building . . . feel certain of their custom and they not only neglect their business here but . . . neither the materials which they use nor the workmen whom they employ here are the best.

(Principal Librarian,'
27 September 1856)

27 SATURDAY • 1945 Duke of Portland agrees to the Museum's purchase of the Portland Vase •

GIFTS 1764

"A piece of eccentric turning in ivory: from Ephr. Reinhold Seehl of Poplar"

28 SUNDAY • 1994 Opening of the Hirayama Conservation Studio •

King Edwards VII's galleries under construction, 1910; Frank Lishman.

29 MONDAY • 1995 Gift from The British Museum Company Ltd for the Great Court •

'The British Museum is the illustration of the history of civilization – no less. In view of the stupendous field that is covered it is clear that it would take a lifetime of study thoroughly to appreciate its treasures.'

(Margaret E. Tabor,
*Round the British Museum:
A Beginner's Guide*, 1927)

30 TUESDAY

1 WEDNESDAY

September 2003

MON	TUES	WED	THUR	FRI	SAT	SUN
1	2	3	4	5	6	7
8	9	10	11	12	13	14
15	16	17	18	19	20	21
22	23	24	25	26	27	28
29	30					

October 2003

MON	TUES	WED	THUR	FRI	SAT	SUN
		1	2	3	4	5
6	7	8	9	10	11	12
13	14	15	16	17	18	19
20	21	22	23	24	25	26
27	28	29	30	31		

2 THURSDAY – ◑

2003

GIFTS 1760

"An Account of the Society
for the encouragement
of British troops. Lond. 1759
in 8o. By that Society"

3 FRIDAY — UNITY DAY, GERMANY
• 1831 King's Library briefly opened to the public •

4 SATURDAY

5 SUNDAY • 1869 Death from cholera at Shiraz, Persia, of Claudius James Richard, diplomat, orientalist and archaeologist •

'This morning the marble statue of Shakespeare executed by Roubiliac in 1758 was placed upon its pedestal in the hall of the British Museum. This statue was bequeathed to the Museum by David Garrick Esqr.'

(Diary of Thomas Conrath, 30 September 1823)

Entance Hall, Montague House; George Scharf the Elder, 1845. Roubiliac's Shakespeare is on the right.

6   MONDAY • 1869 Queen Victoria donates an Easter Island Statue (Hoa Hakananai'a) •

Statue from Easter Island,
Hoa Hakananai'a.

GIFTS 1775

*"A collection of artificial curiosities
from the South Sea Islands: from
Captain Cook"*

7   TUESDAY

GIFTS 1773

*"A Fox, stuffed, from the Falkland
Island: from Dr William Hunter"*

8   WEDNESDAY • 1908 Ezra Pound obtains a reader's ticket •

October 2003

MON	TUES	WED	THUR	FRI	SAT	SUN
		1	2	3	4	5
6	7	8	9	10	11	12
13	14	15	16	17	18	19
20	21	22	23	24	25	26
27	28	29	30	31		

9   THURSDAY

November 2003

MON	TUES	WED	THUR	FRI	SAT	SUN
					1	2
3	4	5	6	7	8	9
10	11	12	13	14	15	16
17	18	19	20	21	22	23
24	25	26	27	28	29	30

10 FRIDAY — ○

---

11 SATURDAY • 1958 Gift of funds to acquire the Ilbert horological collection reported •

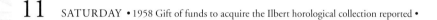

The Mildenhall Dish, Rome, 4th century AD.

12 SUNDAY — NATIONAL DAY, SPAIN
• 1895 Acquisition of the Malcolm collection of Old Master drawings approved • 1946 Acquisition of the Mildenhall treasure approved •

'Among the many and great advantages, which must necessarily accrue to the public from the establishment of the British Museum, this may justly be esteemed not the least considerable; that it provides a safe and lasting repository for curiosities of every kind, whether of art or nature, accessible to all persons in their researches into any parts of useful knowledge. The want of this has been hitherto much lamented not only by learned men, as a great impediment to the progress of science, but likewise by many persons possessed of such curiosities, who have been often at a loss, how and where to reposite them for the benefit of posterity.'

(Original papers, 1756)

13 MONDAY • 1928 Division of finds from Ur; the Museum acquires the Standard and the Royal Game of Ur •

14 TUESDAY

'A reader,
Mr J.B.E., had been
found smoking
in one of the closets
attached to
the Reading Room,
for which offence
he had subsequently
expressed regret.

(Standing Committee,'
14 October 1882)

15 WEDNESDAY

October 2003

MON	TUES	WED	THUR	FRI	SAT	SUN
		1	2	3	4	5
6	7	8	9	10	11	12
13	14	15	16	17	18	19
20	21	22	23	24	25	26
27	28	29	30	31		

November 2003

MON	TUES	WED	THUR	FRI	SAT	SUN
					1	2
3	4	5	6	7	8	9
10	11	12	13	14	15	16
17	18	19	20	21	22	23
24	25	26	27	28	29	30

16 THURSDAY

17 FRIDAY

18 SATURDAY — ◑

19 SUNDAY

Photograph of Discobolus with the Egyptian Sculpture Gallery in the background; Roger Fenton, 1857.

THE BRITISH MUSEUM IN THE TWENTY-FIRST CENTURY

The experience of today's visitor is dominated by the gleaming silver and white of the Queen Elizabeth II Great Court, opened in December 2000 as the Museum's Millennium project. The national library has gone to St Pancras and the gilded Reading Room, haunted by the shades of Karl Marx and other revolutionaries, appears as it was when it first opened in 1857, but is now open to all.

A major transformation took place towards the end of the previous century. Behind the high walls of the Great Court can be found Egyptian mummies and coffins no longer in serried ranks against the dingy walls but in enormous glass cases. The oriental collection displayed in the King Edward building in the vast Joseph E. Hotung gallery, its walls covered with gold leaf, is stunning. The Amaravati sculptures, long hidden in a basement, are fully visible in an air-conditioned room at the end of the gallery. Roman Britain, now housed in the upper eastern range of galleries, is a sparkling treasure trove demonstrating the previously relatively unknown wealth of the province of Britain. The adjacent 18th- and 19th-century European galleries also glitter. The display arranged by the Department of Coins and Medals is quite transformed from the dry series of British coins – a 'temporary' exhibition which lasted for many years, into a fascinating display on 'Money'. In the range of three classical galleries on the upper western floor Smirke's ceiling has been recreated after its destruction by bombing during the War and there are displays on the Roman Empire, the Etruscans, Cyprus and Italy before the Romans. Prints and drawings have a modern gallery where Old Master drawings and the most modern works of art can be seen. Japanese antiquities are displayed in a new gallery created in what was the attic of King Edward VII's galleries. The Ancient Near Eastern galleries have also been transformed and the departmental staff and their collections are now housed in one of the Museum's finest private interiors – Robert Smirke's Arched Room. The first new galleries heralding the return of the Ethnography collection to Bloomsbury

from Burlington Gardens have appeared, displaying Mexican, North American and African collections.

The Museum begins the 21st century, as it has so many decades, with a shortage of funds. Just after its foundation, in 1759, the poet Thomas Gray wrote, '[The Trustees] have £900 a year income, and spend 1300 . . . I expect in winter to see the collection advertised and set to auction'. This pessimistic warning has been repeated many times. But the Museum

The Queen Elizabeth II Great Court at night.

has survived, for it has a capacity both to reinvent itself to meet contemporary needs while at the same time retaining its core values. Perhaps it epitomizes the attitude of one of the memorable characters invented by a famous user of the Museum's reading room, Charles Dickens's Mr Micawber, for whom something always turned up.

2003

GIFTS 1778

"A Collection of artificial curiosities from the South Sea Islands from Joseph Banks Esqre"

20 MONDAY • 1815 Acquisition of the Phigaleian Marbles (the Bassae frieze) •

'**I**f any Person chuses to snarl, bite, or Criticise this Performance, if with Candour we will submit; wishing, however, if they seek for Errors, that they would not give any instance of them in this Work . . . for the Author is one of those who has deserved a better Fate, having all his life seen the back of Fortune, gone up Hill and rowed against the Stream'

(J. and A. van Rymsdyk, *Museum Britannicum*)

21 TUESDAY

22 WEDNESDAY

October 2003

MON	TUES	WED	THUR	FRI	SAT	SUN
		1	2	3	4	5
6	7	8	9	10	11	12
13	14	15	16	17	18	19
20	21	22	23	24	25	26
27	28	29	30	31		

November 2003

MON	TUES	WED	THUR	FRI	SAT	SUN
					1	2
3	4	5	6	7	8	9
10	11	12	13	14	15	16
17	18	19	20	21	22	23
24	25	26	27	28	29	30

23 THURSDAY • 1731 Cotton Library damaged by fire at Asburnham House, Little Dean's yard, Westminster •

---

24 FRIDAY — UNITED NATIONS DAY

---

25 SATURDAY — ● • 1975 Acquisition of the Water Newton treasure sanctioned • 1997 Closure of the round Reading Room by the British Library •

GIFTS 1759

"The Web of a Silkworm wrought in the form of a ribband with an attested Narrative of the fact: from the Viscountess Kilmurry"

26 SUNDAY — NATIONAL DAY, AUSTRIA; BRITISH SUMMER TIME ENDS; SUMMER TIME ENDS (EU)

'Took a stroll over the British Museum, which I had not seen since the new buildings – Went up the old Staircase with painted walls and ceiling, with the 2 old Stuffed Cameleopards going to decay, into the room containing feathered idols of hideous aspect & clubs, weapons, utensils & canoes of various Savage nations looking just as they used to do when I, a tiny Urchin of 8 years of age, first saw them.'

(Diary of W.E. Maxwell, 23 October 1833)

GIFTS 1769

*"An Occidental Bezoar from the
Stomach of a Deer: from Dr Tyffe
of George Town, South Carolina"*

27 MONDAY — HOLIDAY (R. OF IRELAND)

GIFTS 1769

*"A Pebble of the Figure
of a Pear found in a Field near
Stonehenge from Mr Wm Burnly
of Amesbury, Wiltshire"*

28 TUESDAY

29 WEDNESDAY

30 THURSDAY

October 2003

MON	TUES	WED	THUR	FRI	SAT	SUN
		1	2	3	4	5
6	7	8	9	10	11	12
13	14	15	16	17	18	19
20	21	22	23	24	25	26
27	28	29	30	31		

November 2003

MON	TUES	WED	THUR	FRI	SAT	SUN
					1	2
3	4	5	6	7	8	9
10	11	12	13	14	15	16
17	18	19	20	21	22	23
24	25	26	27	28	29	30

2003

31 FRIDAY — HALLOWE'EN

• 2000 Gift from the Ford Motor Company for the Ford Centre for Young Visitors •

1 SATURDAY — ◗

2 SUNDAY

Francis Douce, reasons for resigning from the Museum, 1811 …

• The vastness of the business remaining to be done & continually flowing in.

• The total impossibility of my individual efforts, limited, restrained & controuled as they are, to do any real, or at least much, good …

• The want of society with the members, their habits wholly different & their manners far from fascinating & sometimes repulsive …

• Their [the Trustees] fiddle faddle requisition of incessant reports, the greatest part of which can inform them of nothing, or, when they do, of what they are generally incapable of understanding or fairly judging.   (Bodleian Library MSS Douce.e.28)

2003

3   MONDAY

'**O**rdered, That the
Minute of the Trustees . . .
directing 'That no Dogs
or Poultry be kept within
the Museum' be
communicated to all
officers and persons
residing in the Museum,
for their guidance.'

(Principal Librarian,
9 November 1861)

4   TUESDAY • 1994 Opening of the Mexican Gallery •

5   WEDNESDAY — GUY FAWKES

November 2003

MON	TUES	WED	THUR	FRI	SAT	SUN
					1	2
3	4	5	6	7	8	9
10	11	12	13	14	15	16
17	18	19	20	21	22	23
24	25	26	27	28	29	30

December 2003

MON	TUES	WED	THUR	FRI	SAT	SUN
1	2	3	4	5	6	7
8	9	10	11	12	13	14
15	16	17	18	19	20	21
22	23	24	25	26	27	28
29	30	31				

6   THURSDAY

2003

GIFTS 1785

*'A hornet's nest found in Yorkshire:
from Mr Burroughs'*

7 FRIDAY

GIFTS 1776

*'A very valuable Collection
of Antiquities
from Sir William Hamilton'*

8 SATURDAY • 2000 Opening of the Korea Foundation Gallery •

9 SUNDAY — ○ • 1992 Opening of The Joseph E. Hotung Gallery of Oriental Antiquities •

'I had slept little during the night. . . . Hopes, long cherished, were now to be realised, or were to end in disappointment. Visions of palaces under-ground, of gigantic monsters, of sculptured figures, and endless inscriptions, floated before me. After forming plan after plan for removing the earth and extricating the treasures, I fancied myself wandering in a maze of chambers from which I could find no outlet. Then, again, all was reburied, and I was standing on the grass-covered mound.'

(Layard arrives at Nimrud, 8 November 1845)

Discovery of a colossal Assyrian head at Nimrud.

A 'Prudhoe lion'.

10 MONDAY • 1834 Lord Prudhoe offers to donate two granite lions from Gebel Barkal, Sudan •

11 TUESDAY — VETERANS DAY
• 1848 Acquisition of the Black Obelisk of Shalmaneser •

'Ordered, That neither the watchmen, nor any other person be permitted to carry a dog into the garden.'

(Standing Committee, 12 November 1756)

12 WEDNESDAY • 1831 Purchase of the Lewis chessmen approved •

November 2003

MON	TUES	WED	THUR	FRI	SAT	SUN
					1	2
3	4	5	6	7	8	9
10	11	12	13	14	15	16
17	18	19	20	21	22	23
24	25	26	27	28	29	30

December 2003

MON	TUES	WED	THUR	FRI	SAT	SUN
1	2	3	4	5	6	7
8	9	10	11	12	13	14
15	16	17	18	19	20	21
22	23	24	25	26	27	28
29	30	31				

13 THURSDAY • 1995 Gift from the Monument Trust for the Great Court •

GIFTS 1762

"A piece of Lace made of the hair of Queen Elizabeth: from Miss Revell of Watling Street"

14 FRIDAY

15 SATURDAY • 1994 Launch of the 250th Anniversary Development Programme •

GIFTS 1763

"A China bowl disfigured by Fire occasioned by the earthquake at Lisbon, and dug out of the ruins two years after"

16 SUNDAY

'We were once haunted by a shabby-genteel man; he was bodily present to our senses all day, and he was in our mind's eye all night . . . He first attracted our notice, by sitting opposite to us in the reading-room at the British Museum; and what made the man more remarkable was, that he always had before him a couple of shabby-genteel books – two old dogs-eared folios, in mouldy worm-eaten covers, which had once been smart.'

(Charles Dickens, *Sketches by Boz*, 1836)

2003

*"An Account of the general
Contents of the British Museum
printed Lond. 1761 8o
presented by Mr Dodsley"*

17 MONDAY — ◑

18 TUESDAY • 1905 The novelist and essayist Virginia Woolf obtains a reader's ticket •

12: '**T**HAT no children
be admitted
into the Museum.'

(Statutes and Rules 1757)

19 WEDNESDAY

November 2003

MON	TUES	WED	THUR	FRI	SAT	SUN
					1	2
3	4	5	6	7	8	9
10	11	12	13	14	15	16
17	18	19	20	21	22	23
24	25	26	27	28	29	30

20 THURSDAY

December 2003

MON	TUES	WED	THUR	FRI	SAT	SUN
1	2	3	4	5	6	7
8	9	10	11	12	13	14
15	16	17	18	19	20	21
22	23	24	25	26	27	28
29	30	31				

21   FRIDAY

22   SATURDAY • 1833 The poet Robert Browning obtains a reader's ticket •

'This splendid national
Institution …'
(*The People's Handbook to the
British Museum*, 1843)

23   SUNDAY — ● • 1999 Gift of £1.5 million from BP plc for the BP Lecture Theatre •

British Museum
Officials refusing to
accept a Collection;
George Morrow, 1913.

GIFTS 1763

*"Ten different Saxon Coins
found in 1759 near Peterborough:
by Mr John White
of Newgate Street"*

24 MONDAY

25 TUESDAY

GIFTS 1766

*"Several natural and artificial
curiosities collected
by Commodore Byron in the
Course of his voyage round the
world and Presented by him"*

26 WEDNESDAY • 1753 Draw begins in the British Museum lottery •

27 THURSDAY

November 2003

MON	TUES	WED	THUR	FRI	SAT	SUN
					1	2
3	4	5	6	7	8	9
10	11	12	13	14	15	16
17	18	19	20	21	22	23
24	25	26	27	28	29	30

December 2003

MON	TUES	WED	THUR	FRI	SAT	SUN
1	2	3	4	5	6	7
8	9	10	11	12	13	14
15	16	17	18	19	20	21
22	23	24	25	26	27	28
29	30	31				

2003

NOVEMBER

28 FRIDAY • 1877 Karl Marx obtains his last renewal of his reader's ticket •

29 SATURDAY

30 SUNDAY — ST ANDREW; ADVENT SUNDAY ◗

'Thither Marx drove us. To learn! To learn! . . . While the rest of the fugitives were laying plans for the overthrow of the world and intoxicating themselves day by day, evening by evening, with the hasheesh-drink of "Tomorrow it will start!" – we . . . were sitting in the British Museum and trying to educate ourselves and to prepare arms and ammunition for the battles of the future.'

(Wilhelm Liebknecht, 1901)

Karl Marx (1818–83).

2003

DECEMBER

1 MONDAY

2 TUESDAY • 1996 First British Library books leave Bloomsbury for St Pancras •

3 WEDNESDAY

4 THURSDAY

December 2003

MON	TUES	WED	THUR	FRI	SAT	SUN
1	2	3	4	5	6	7
8	9	10	11	12	13	14
15	16	17	18	19	20	21
22	23	24	25	26	27	28
29	30	31				

January 2004

MON	TUES	WED	THUR	FRI	SAT	SUN
			1	2	3	4
5	6	7	8	9	10	11
12	13	14	15	16	17	18
19	20	21	22	23	24	25
26	27	28	29	30	31	

GIFTS 1767

"A Piece of Writing containing the Creed, the Lords Prayer, and the fourth and following Commandments, in the Compass of a silver penny: from Mr William Isaac Blanchard"

'The Museum
was not opened on
Sunday, 4th December,
on account of fog.'
(Standing Committee,
10 December 1927)

5 FRIDAY • 1896 Sun Yat-Sen, revolutionary, obtains a reader's ticket •

6 SATURDAY — INDEPENDENCE DAY, FINLAND
• 2000 Queen Elizabeth II Great Court opened by the Queen •

7 SUNDAY

'An anthem that Mozart composed on a visit to the British Museum in 1765 was sung last night as the Queen arrived for the official opening of the £100 million Great court. . . . Lord Foster's redesign has transformed the museum's two-acre inner courtyard into the largest covered public square in Europe. Declaring it open, the Queen said: "In the life of the nation, the British Museum is a remarkable phenomenon . . . it is an endless source of learning, inspiration and pleasure for millions of people who visit every year."'

(*The Times*, 7 December 2000)

8 MONDAY — ○ • 1866 Acquisition of the Blacas collection including the Esquiline Treasure •
• 1997 Gift from Sir Joseph Hotung for the Joseph Hotung Great Court Gallery •

The Projecta Casket
from the Esquiline Treasure,
Rome, 4th century AD.

9 TUESDAY • 1987 Opening of the AG Leventis Gallery of Cypriot Antiquities •

'Dr Haas' illness had
been caused by the
'unwholesome condition'
of his room in the
Department of Printed
Books.'

(Standing Committee,
10 December 1881)

10 WEDNESDAY

December 2003

MON	TUES	WED	THUR	FRI	SAT	SUN
1	2	3	4	5	6	7
8	9	10	11	12	13	14
15	16	17	18	19	20	21
22	23	24	25	26	27	28
29	30	31				

January 2004

MON	TUES	WED	THUR	FRI	SAT	SUN
			1	2	3	4
5	6	7	8	9	10	11
12	13	14	15	16	17	18
19	20	21	22	23	24	25
26	27	28	29	30	31	

11 THURSDAY • 1753 First meeting of the Museum Trustees in the Great Room at the Duke of
Newcastle's Office at the Cockpit, Whitehall •

2003

DECEMBER

GIFTS 1794

"One of the first Cups made by the Convicts at Botany Bay with an undescribed Lizard from the same place: from Sir Joseph Banks"

12 FRIDAY • 1753 Final accounts of the British Museum lottery presented to Parliament •

13 SATURDAY

14 SUNDAY

'Sir; although the enquiry proposed by my Hon. Friend is, in my opinion, not only reasonable but necessary, yet I foresaw and expected that it would be opposed; for both from history and experience we may learn, that parliamentary enquiries into the conduct of any officers employed under the crown, high or low, have always been opposed by ministers and their favourites; and if at any time they found themselves forced to submit, they have too often found means to defeat, in a great measure, the effect of the enquiry.'

(Nicholas Fazakerly, MP, Parliamentary debate on the Museum lottery, 1753)

'Dr Watson having reported that one of the weights of the Clock had fallen quite through the Floor of the Clockroom down into the Colonnade and in the fall had shattered to pieces one of the lamps fixed in the Gateway.'

(Standing Committee, 18 December 1767)

15 MONDAY

16 TUESDAY — ☽ • 1897 Vladimir L'vovich Burtsev arrested at the entrance to the Reading Room for soliciting the murder of the Tsar of Russia •

17 WEDNESDAY

18 THURSDAY • 1898 Death of Baron Ferdinand James Rothschild and bequest of *objets d'art* from the New Smoking Room at Waddesdon manor • 1920 The author of the Peter Wimsey stories, Dorothy L. Sayers, obtains a reader's ticket •

December 2003

MON	TUES	WED	THUR	FRI	SAT	SUN
1	2	3	4	5	6	7
8	9	10	11	12	13	14
15	16	17	18	19	20	21
22	23	24	25	26	27	28
29	30	31				

January 2004

MON	TUES	WED	THUR	FRI	SAT	SUN
			1	2	3	4
5	6	7	8	9	10	11
12	13	14	15	16	17	18
19	20	21	22	23	24	25
26	27	28	29	30	31	

19　FRIDAY

20　SATURDAY

'Complaint having
been made by some of the
Duke of Bedford's Family
that the corners of the
Great Gate of the Museum
were not kept clean.'

(Standing Committee,
18 December 1767)

21　SUNDAY

'It is to be observed in general that owing to the vigilance & strictness of the Police, the lower Classes in France are habituated to a far more orderly behaviour than ours, abundance of individuals being observed among our popular Visitors who, in the fervour of independence, pride themselves in shewing a disdain of order, & in doing essential mischief . . . Mr P. is informed by a gentleman of undoubted veracity, lately return'd from Paris, that the only instance hitherto observed of any trespass at their public exhibitions, was committed by two Englishmen. With us, three instances of mutilation, not very material indeed, have occurred within these few months.'

(Principal Librarian, 1814)

2003

*"A Limpet with the fish
sticking to it . . .
from James Theobalds Esqre"*

22 MONDAY

23 TUESDAY — EMPEROR'S BIRTHDAY, JAPAN ●

ORDER 1762

*"A map of the Indian Nations
north west of S. Carolina, copied
from an original Indian Map,
presented to Governor Nicholson:
from Dr Maty"*

24 WEDNESDAY • 1881 Henry Hook VC of Rorke's Drift appointed an 'Inside Duster' •

December 2003

MON	TUES	WED	THUR	FRI	SAT	SUN
1	2	3	4	5	6	7
8	9	10	11	12	13	14
15	16	17	18	19	20	21
22	23	24	25	26	27	28
29	30	31				

January 2004

MON	TUES	WED	THUR	FRI	SAT	SUN
			1	2	3	4
5	6	7	8	9	10	11
12	13	14	15	16	17	18
19	20	21	22	23	24	25
26	27	28	29	30	31	

25 THURSDAY — CHRISTMAS DAY, HOLIDAY (UK AND R. OF IRELAND)

2003

DECEMBER

26 FRIDAY — BOXING DAY, HOLIDAY (UK AND R. OF IRELAND)
• 1859 Acquisition of the Demeter of Knidos • 1841 Charles Fellows's excavation party lands at the mouth of the Xanthos River •

27 SATURDAY

28 SUNDAY

'Staid at home for fear of mischief from the Holiday people who visited us today to the number of more than 8800. We had eight of the Metropolitan Police scattered about our rooms to assist in protecting us.'

(Diary of Sir Henry Ellis, 26 December 1838)

The Demeter of Knidos
in the Mausoleum Room;
George Goodwin Kilburne, *c.* 1880.

2003/4

'Idle or Employd, I always think a Library the best of Rooms to sit in.'

(Talleyrand on a visit to the Museum 29 December 1832)

GIFTS 1758

"A remarkable Bird's Nest: from Mr Colebrooke"

29 MONDAY

30 TUESDAY — ☽ • 1914 The poet T.S. Eliot obtains a reader's ticket •

31 WEDNESDAY

1 THURSDAY — NEW YEAR'S DAY, HOLIDAY (UK AND R. OF IRELAND)

December 2003

MON	TUES	WED	THUR	FRI	SAT	SUN
1	2	3	4	5	6	7
8	9	10	11	12	13	14
15	16	17	18	19	20	21
22	23	24	25	26	27	28
29	30	31				

January 2004

MON	TUES	WED	THUR	FRI	SAT	SUN
			1	2	3	4
5	6	7	8	9	10	11
12	13	14	15	16	17	18
19	20	21	22	23	24	25
26	27	28	29	30	31	

'I do Will and desire that for the promoting of these noble ends, the glory of God, and the good of man, my collection in all its branches may be, if possible kept and preserved together whole and intire.'

(Codicil to the Will
of Sir Hans Sloane, 1749)

2 FRIDAY — HOLIDAY (SCOTLAND)

3 SATURDAY • 1805 Death of Charles Townley •

4 SUNDAY

The Museum in winter, 1991.

ADDRESSES

NAME

ADDRESS

TEL.

MOBILE

E-MAIL

FAX

NAME

ADDRESS

TEL.

MOBILE

E-MAIL

FAX

NAME

ADDRESS

TEL.

MOBILE

E-MAIL

FAX

NAME

ADDRESS

TEL.

MOBILE

E-MAIL

FAX

NAME

ADDRESS

TEL.

MOBILE

E-MAIL

FAX

NAME

ADDRESS

TEL.

MOBILE

E-MAIL

FAX

NAME

ADDRESS

TEL.

MOBILE

E-MAIL

FAX

NAME

ADDRESS

TEL.

MOBILE

E-MAIL

FAX

NAME

ADDRESS

TEL.

MOBILE

E-MAIL

FAX

NAME

ADDRESS

TEL.

MOBILE

E-MAIL

FAX

NAME

ADDRESS

TEL.

MOBILE

E-MAIL

FAX

NAME

ADDRESS

TEL.

MOBILE

E-MAIL

FAX

NAME

ADDRESS

TEL.

MOBILE

E-MAIL

FAX

NAME

ADDRESS

TEL.

MOBILE

E-MAIL

FAX

NAME

ADDRESS

TEL.

MOBILE

E-MAIL

FAX

NAME

ADDRESS

TEL.

MOBILE

E-MAIL

FAX

NAME

ADDRESS

TEL.

MOBILE

E-MAIL

FAX

NAME

ADDRESS

TEL.

MOBILE

E-MAIL

FAX

NAME

ADDRESS

TEL.

MOBILE

E-MAIL

FAX

NAME

ADDRESS

TEL.

MOBILE

E-MAIL

FAX

NAME

ADDRESS

TEL.

MOBILE

E-MAIL

FAX

NAME

ADDRESS

TEL.

MOBILE

E-MAIL

FAX

NAME

ADDRESS

TEL.

MOBILE

E-MAIL

FAX

NAME

ADDRESS

TEL.

MOBILE

E-MAIL

FAX

NAME

ADDRESS

TEL.

MOBILE

E-MAIL

FAX

NAME

ADDRESS

TEL.

MOBILE

E-MAIL

FAX

NAME

ADDRESS

TEL.

MOBILE

E-MAIL

FAX

NAME

ADDRESS

TEL.

MOBILE

E-MAIL

FAX

NAME

ADDRESS

TEL.

MOBILE

E-MAIL

FAX

NAME

ADDRESS

TEL.

MOBILE

E-MAIL

FAX

NAME

ADDRESS

TEL.

MOBILE

E-MAIL

FAX

NAME

ADDRESS

TEL.

MOBILE

E-MAIL

FAX

NAME

ADDRESS

TEL.

MOBILE

E-MAIL

FAX

NAME

ADDRESS

TEL.

MOBILE

E-MAIL

FAX

NAME

ADDRESS

TEL.

MOBILE

E-MAIL

FAX

NAME

ADDRESS

TEL.

MOBILE

E-MAIL

FAX

NAME

ADDRESS

TEL.

MOBILE

E-MAIL

FAX

NAME

ADDRESS

TEL.

MOBILE

E-MAIL

FAX

NAME

ADDRESS

TEL.

MOBILE

E-MAIL

FAX

NAME

ADDRESS

TEL.

MOBILE

E-MAIL

FAX

Text written and compiled by Marjorie Caygill

First published in 2002 by The British Museum Press
A division of The British Museum Company Ltd
46 Bloomsbury Street, London WC1B 3QQ

ISBN 0 7141 27736

Designed by Harry Green
Typeset in Garamond
Printed in Spain by Grafos SA

ACKNOWLEDGEMENTS

Excerpts from The Diary of Sir Henry Ellis (weeks
commencing 27 January, 24 March, 7 July and
22 December) and The Diary of Thomas Conrath
(week commencing 29 September) © British Library
(Add. MS. 36,653 and Add. MS. 58207).

Excerpts from The Diary of Sir Frederic Madden
(weeks commencing 3 February, 24 March,
7 April and 19 May) and Francis Douce (week
commencing 27 October) © Bodleian Library,
Oxford (MSS Eng. hist. *c*.140–82 and
MSS Douce.e.28).

Extract from 'The British Museum Reading Room'
(week commencing 14 April) taken from Louis
MacNeice's *Collected Poems*, reproduced courtesy
of Faber & Faber.

Cartoon from *The Comic News* (week commencing
26 May) and Mozart's 'God is our Refuge' (week
commencing 14 July) © British Library.

Photograph of the British Museum Act and Trustees'
Mace (week commencing 2 June) by Lee Boltin.

Illustration of lottery ticket (week commencing
9 June) © Wellcome Institute for the History
of Medicine.

Photograph of the British Museum in winter (week
commencing 29 December) by Geoffrey House.